BOOMERS TO
MILLENNIALS

Boomers to Millennials calmly and reasonably makes the case for a progressive America. With bullseye accuracy, the authors take on all the subterfuge created by the right-wing machine and offer a countervision that stays within the lines of facts, reality and action. With the Boomer's knowledge of the backstory, and the Millennial's savvy, open-minded approach, the lessons in this book could be just the thing that stops the corporate greed that's eviscerating America.

Heidi Siegmund Cuda
Emmy award-winning investigative reporter,
filmmaker, author, and activist

★★

This clarion call is a must read for all voters, but especially the young. We're seeing a rebirth of activism in this country, but we need millennials to save America from the excesses of Donald Trump allowed or encouraged by older voters. *Boomers to Millennials* is a how to guide to a better, more inclusive nation.

John Weaver
Chief Strategist for former Senator John McCain
and Governor John Kasich

★★

BOOMERS TO MILLENNIALS

★★ *Moving America Forward* ★★

Daniel R. Rubin & Nathan H. Rubin

Bardolf & Company
Sarasota, Florida

Bardolf & Company

BOOMERS TO MILLENNIALS
Moving America Forward

ISBN 978-1-938842-41-2

Published by Bardolf & Company
5430 Colewood Pl.
Sarasota, FL 34232
941-232-0113
www.bardolfandcompany.com

Cover design by Sarah Sosland
*   and Catleen Shaw, http//www.shawcreative.com*

Cover photo of Daniel R. Rubin by Shellie Rubin
Cover photo of Nathan H. Rubin by Mustache Agency:,
*   https://www.mustacheagency.com/*

To Hashem,

Our Family,

The Founders and Framers who created this
Great Nation of ours,

And to all those working
to form a more perfect union.

TABLE OF CONTENTS

A nation that is afraid to let its people judge the truth and falsehood in an open market is a nation that is afraid of its people.

—John F. Kennedy

INTRODUCTION

The Boomer and the Millennial

A Boomer and a Millennial, who happen to be father and son, wrote this book because they share a vision for America, based on our great history and shaped by the events both have witnessed and experienced.

For the Boomer, his first pertinent recollections occurred the day President John F. Kennedy was shot when he wondered why so many people were so visibly upset. Other important experiences soon followed—notably the televised war in Vietnam, the assassinations of Martin Luther King Jr., and Robert Kennedy, and various NASA missions to the moon. The Boomer also saw our government tested as never before during the constitutional crisis created by President Richard Nixon shortly before he resigned. The lessons of Watergate and its aftermath made a huge impact on the Boomer. So did the rise of the Evangelical Right in more recent years, enabled by partisan talk radio and Fox News, facing the reality that in the near future America's white citizens will no longer be in the majority. Their attempts to subvert our democratic institutions of government in response have been deeply troubling.

The Millennial, always reminded of our history and the experiences of the Boomer, vividly recalls the most heinous foreign attack on American soil since Pearl Harbor—September 11 in 2001. He grew up acutely aware of two wars, in Iraq and Afghanistan, and the ensuing collapse of Wall Street and our financial institutions which nearly toppled our economic system. In 2008, he witnessed the election of Barack Obama and thought the world had finally begun to change for the better.

With the 2016 elections and the continuing specter of destructive and potentially treasonous actions by the Trump Campaign and President Donald Trump himself, both Boomer and Millennial felt an urgency to do something. They decided to write about what the Boomers have contributed to society in their time and how important it is now for the Millennials to take the lead and advance their collective vision of a progressive, economically strong, and democratic America in the 21st century.

The Boomer and the Millennial both believe in personal freedom, but also appreciate the positive role government can play in our modern society. They both believe that America is ready to take the next steps forward. But it will not happen unless greater numbers of citizens than are currently engaged become active participants in the process.

More from the Boomer

Several years ago, I attended a forum with other educators to discuss how we each introduce American history to new students. Being the "new" guy in the group, I waited my turn to speak and when asked, I started, "History repeats itself"—and was cut off by the senior member of the group. Her retort was short and sharp: "You can't tell students this—it will give them no hope!" I replied, "If you teach them that history repeats itself, they should be able to identify the circumstances that resulted in the undesired outcomes and if they can anticipate those outcomes, they should be able to change those circumstances so that we don't make the same mistakes over again."

I have long been an avid advocate for requiring students to achieve at the highest levels of critical thinking and application. By learning the entire "mosaic" of history (providing more than a thumbnail's sketch), they are better equipped to identify analogous trends and change the outcomes for Americans of all ages and backgrounds who lack a general understanding and appreciation of our history. They don't realize that our country, as we know it, would not exist without the involvement of concerned citizens, from its founding over 200 years ago to today. To that end, I have provided historical context for many of the issues addressed in this book.

As we witness the chaos and upheaval in the world created by the ideologues whose "America First" approach abdicates the essential leadership role our country has played since at least 1900, I began to think about the necessity of Baby Boomers finally ceding leadership authority to those that follow—the Millennials! I believe that now is the time for the younger generation to step up and begin to participate fully in our electoral affairs. We Boomers had our chance and we accomplished many good things, yet the work never ends in an evolving world as new issues arise, requiring new thinking and solutions.

In an effort to make this "transition" of leadership authority, I am blessed to be able to work with my son Nathan, who is passionately engaged in activating Millennials to "step up" and accept responsibility for the future of our great democracy.

Nathan, as Founder and CEO of *Millennial Politics* (a group dedicated to promoting a positive agenda for Millennials to change the world through activism and elected office), is in a unique position to reflect on the concerns of Millennials and what steps they can and should take to begin the process of obtaining leadership authority through the democratic process. The emergence of a new crop of young, energetic and active Americans willing to move this country forward in the 21st Century is an exciting development, and I am pleased to support it in whatever way I can.

More from the Millennial

As a child of the 1990s and product of the public-school systems in Ohio and Florida, I grew up in an upper-middle-class home. I didn't have to worry about violence on my way to and from school, or wonder where my next meal would come from, or whether my parents would come home at night. By any measure, I lived an idyllic childhood in a stable, dual-income family, with a roof over my head, a fenced-in backyard, and a strong community surrounding me.

By the time I came to realize others were not so fortunate, that there was a world full of bigotry, injustice, pain, and poverty for many, the United States was already involved in two wars and on the brink of the greatest economic recession in generations. It was in the run-up to the election of Barack Obama in 2008 that I began to read, question, and find my voice. Having turned 18 in May of 2008, this was my first election as an eligible voter, and I paid close attention to the choices at-hand.

Watching Senator John McCain, Sarah Palin and their surrogates on the campaign trail was a fascinating and troubling experience. I'd observe their bad-faith attacks in disbelief and wonder, "This can't really be how national politicians are supposed to act, right?" Shortly before the election, in a now famous interview, a journalist asked Palin what newspapers she read. She couldn't even name one. I was shocked. I had begun following the news and could name at least a half-dozen publications I dug into on a regular basis (many of which are cited in this book), including *The Washington Post, The New York Times, Huffington Post*, POLITICO, *The Wall Street Journal, Times of Israel*, etc. As the campaign went on, I became increasingly frustrated about the disgust with which Palin and the GOP regarded the "experts" and the "elite." In retrospect, it marked the beginning of Republicans moving into rampant anti-intellectualism during a presidential campaign, foreshadowing the rise of Trumpism.

While attending college, I remained attuned to current events, although I didn't do much to actively influence them. I was focused on school, and slept well at night knowing President Obama had professionals working on the issues. It wasn't until after I graduated and moved to New York City in 2012 that I began to become more involved in the "next generation" political space. Groups like Run for America, Action for America, No Labels, The Centrist Project, and others started to pop up, and I began to attend their events regularly.

While never working full-time for these groups, I tried my best to help spread the word. I'd text my friends, "Hey! Want to go to this Run For America event?" and they replied affirmatively, followed by "Wtf is Run for America?" Judging by their reactions, I quickly realized there wasn't an enthusiasm gap amongst millennials, there was an awareness gap; my network simply didn't know *how* to get involved politically.

After several years of going to these events and networking in the space, I wanted to do more. So, around the time of the 2016 election, while occasionally knocking on doors and phone banking for Hillary Clinton's Presidential campaign, I started what was ultimately to become *Millennial Politics*.

Since then, *Millennial Politics* has developed a national audience, and we've interviewed and told the stories of hundreds of Democratic candidates up and down the ballot on our website, podcast, social media and livestreams. We've gained more than 100,000 followers across social media, and our content has reached over 60,000,000 people since we started.

Why is this important, and what about this timing made this possible?

We find ourselves living in a world flooded with misinformation, propaganda, and a Right-Wing Media complex propped up by selling fear, xenophobia, and racism to activate their mostly older, mostly white constituents.

Furthermore, Donald Trump's reality show, media savvy style has dominated the news cycle to the point that other politicians or organizations have a difficult time being heard. But that's where digital media has revolutionized how we approach news. And it's changing how political candidates go about getting their messages out. Virality is rapid, unexpected, and generally unstoppable. Millennials, as a generation, are the most equipped to succeed in this new era. Generally speaking, we are digital natives, tech-savvy, comfortable with diversity, embracing of change, and enthusiastic about building a better world.

We are also more embracing of social and cultural developments that make many Boomers uncomfortable, including progressive changes like gay marriage, LGBTQ+ rights, religious tolerance and freedom, marijuana legalization, common-sense Constitutional gun regulation, and Medicare for all.

Progressivism as a political approach isn't a new idea. Figures from our past like Patrick Henry, Thomas Jefferson, Frederick Douglass, Harriet Tubman, Theodore Roosevelt, Frances Perkins, Eleanor Roosevelt, Harry S. Truman, Robert F. Kennedy, Rosa Parks, Dr. Martin Luther King Jr., and others all championed progressive ideas in one form or another. Millennials can (and should) look to them for inspiration and guidance.

I believe that it's time for a new Progressive Era in this country where we choose to value people over profit, climate-friendly power sources over fossil fuels, and come together over our shared values of Life, Liberty, and the Pursuit of Happiness.

★★★★

America has always expected each generation to build upon the achievements of preceding generations and to continue shaping our democracy so that it remains vibrant and active well into the future. Boomers accepted this role from the "Greatest Generation," and now it is time for Millennials to take the torch from Boomers. We hope that this book will help in the transition process by identifying the issues Millennials face and the steps they can take to institute positive changes to our society through advocacy and activism.

If you are reading this book, we hope you will glean enough information to provide the incentive to get involved in your political community. And as capitalists in the tradition of John Locke, the English philosopher whose thinking influenced our Founding Fathers, Founding Mothers and Constitutional Framers, we are pleased that you purchased this book and hope you enjoy it.

Daniel R. Rubin & Nathan H. Rubin
October 2018

★★ PART I ★★

Millennials—
Time to Take the Reins

The people are the only legitimate fountain of power, and it is from them that the constitutional charter, under which the several branches of government hold their power, is derived.

— James Madison

Never doubt that a small group of thoughtful, committed citizens can change the world; indeed, it's the only thing that ever has.

—Margaret Mead

Millennials have gotten a bad rap. Blamed for a wide variety of ills and problems besetting our changing society, they have been vilified, libeled and slandered like no other generation in American history. Just google "Millennials Killed" and you'll be amazed all the things Millennials have supposedly destroyed with their consumption habits and self-centered attitudes—beer, Toys R Us, the housing industry, movies, sex, Buffalo Wild Wings, bar soap, Home Depot, and mayonnaise, to name a few. Some of these allegations are plainly silly; others, like the results of the 2016 election, are more serious accusations, yet equally absurd.

So, who are these up-and-comers rocking the boat, murdering commercial giants, and tearing America's social fabric to pieces?

Millennials are commonly defined as individuals born in the 1980s and 1990s that have or are coming of age in the 21st Century. Yet, unlike previous generations of Americans growing into positions of power and influence, Millennials remain largely ignored by the powers that be in our centers of political influence and control. The Baby Boomers that precede them have solidified their grip on social, economic and political power and remain reluctant to cede any of that authority.

Throughout history, and America is no exception, societies have always been uncomfortable with change brought on by its youthful members, inevitable as it may be. Such change is always unsettling, and older folks often cling to the notion of better times past—the good old days. More than 2,000 years ago, the poet Virgil complained about the pollution, unsafe streets at night, gang violence, and a general increase in rudeness in the city of Rome, in contrast to the "golden era" of his youth. But those backward-looking dreams of better times are illusory, seen through rose-colored glasses that ignore all the difficulties of past times. Society is always changing, and the refusal of America's current leaders to engage and include Millennials comes with its own risk.

So, why is the older generation so reluctant to welcome Millennials to the table? There are a number of claims and rationalizations, all bogus, but presented with enough credence by the media that all-too-many people believe them. They include accusations that Millennials are:

- Too young and inexperienced
- Too cynical and unwilling to get involved
- Too poorly educated
- Too radical in their demands

Let's take a look at them, one at a time.

Too young and inexperienced

The charge against Millennials being too young and inexperienced is so commonplace, there are regular memes about Millennials seeking jobs. Employers want someone to fill an entry-level job, be paid entry-level salaries, yet have at least three to five years previous experience with a college degree, specialized technical skills, and a "commitment to the field."

In order to get ahead, many Millennials have had to take full-time, unpaid internships to "pay their dues" and gain the experience necessary to get their foot in the door in their respective fields. The practice of employers using unpaid internships for college students was recently ruled illegal, but it continues to occur with frequency. Not everyone is able to work for free; only those fortunate enough to receive support from family, friends, or some other arrangement can. This says nothing against those who sought out and received said internships, but it is important to remember that the system in which we operate is inherently discriminatory against those of lesser means.

As we move forward, we can do better. We will never be able to guarantee equality of outcome, nor should that be our goal, but we should do all we can to ensure equality of opportunity—regardless of race, gender, religion, socioeconomic status, or sexual orientation.

As for the contention that Millennials are simply not old enough to deal with the problems we face, you may be surprised to learn that young people have always been at the forefront of American history. George Washington hadn't reached the age of 21 when he was granted a commission by the Governor of Virginia as a major in the army.

Alexander Hamilton volunteered with the Continental Army at the age of 20. He was appointed as a New York representative to the Congress of the Confederation at the age of 27.

Nathan Hale, an American soldier and spy who famously shouted, "Give me Liberty or Give me Death," was 21 when he was executed by the British forces. Thomas Jefferson was 33 when he penned the Declaration of Independence.

Alice Stone Blackwell was 24 when she founded the Woman's Journal on her way to becoming a leader of the American Suffragette Movement. Carrie Chapman Catt was 31 when she organized the National American Woman Suffrage Association. Susan B. Anthony helped found the Woman's Loyal League at age 33 and became a leader in the women's voting rights movement.

And by the way, Martin Luther King Jr., was only 26 when he led the Montgomery Bus Boycott. He received the Nobel Peace Prize at age 35.

We could go on, but we think you get the point.

While none of these people were perfect or always politically correct in retrospect, especially in their personal lives, their positive impact on our collective history and the progress they helped usher in is without question.

Some people argue that the world was different then. They claim the ages of our Founders and Framers and those who came after them were relative to their times, but plenty of people including Benjamin Franklin lived into their 70's then. (Franklin lived to be 84—he was 70 when the upstarts began reshaping our new national government). Boomers also conveniently forget that many of their leaders in the anti-Vietnam War and Civil Rights movements were under 30 when they made their first appearances on the national stage.

Surely, our era is not so different. To dismiss Millennials as "too young" to be fully engaged in politics and social change indicates, at best, an ignorance of history; at worst, self-serving memory loss.

Too cynical and unwilling to get involved

The claim that Millennials are cynical and unwilling to get involved in the political process has some validity, but there are strong reasons why that is the case.

Millennials are the first Americans to come of age in the post-9/11 world with its ongoing war in Afghanistan, already the longest in American history, and the never ending "wars on terror." They entered adulthood and the job market in the midst of the worst global recession—some have called it a depression—since the 1930s, caused by speculative and, in some cases, illegal practices by large banks and other investment firms. These institutions sold subprime mortgages to low-income families and took risky bets on the stock market, counting on the government to bail them out, if all else failed. And it did.

Millennials also experienced first-hand how private lenders, in partnership with the federal government, used them as profit centers, saddling them with immense student debt. Not only did this practice damage Millennial's immediate prospects but it put them on a path of under-employment for years to come. With their future earnings potential shot and their student loans a constant source of worry, they have had little opportunity to buy a car, purchase a home, start a family, travel, or pursue the American Dream.

No wonder Millennials have a distrust of large institutions, public and private. These institutions continually let them down, yet none have been held truly accountable.

At the same time, Millennials have had a front row seat to the constant wrangling between progressive and conservative ideologies, giving them a sour view of politics. Most Millennials grew up in a post-Columbine world, in which school shootings have increased in frequency while the political discourse regarding solutions continues to stagnate. In dealing with climate change, addressing racial discrimination, furthering religious freedom, providing health care access for all citizens, and other important issues, Millennials have observed elected officials fail to act decisively. These so-called "leaders" have been busy kicking the can down the road for far too long.

Yes, all these developments have made some people cynical and turned them off to the political process. Yet many millions of Millennials want to get involved and make positive societal, political and economic impact. They work and demonstrate for social justice in numbers not seen since the 1960s Civil Rights Movements. They just need the tools to get started and demand what is their birthright as Americans in order to build a better future for themselves and others.

Too poorly educated

Millennials have been dismissed or marginalized for lacking proper gravitas and the education necessary to effectuate real change for our society. Like all the generations that preceded them, they certainly include a number of people with uneducated, ill-informed and provincial views. (Many of these opinions and beliefs were actually handed down to them by their Boomer parents, but we're not placing blame here.)

In reality, millions more Millennials are better educated, better informed, and better equipped to opine on issues facing our diverse society than most Boomers today. They embrace science and prefer facts, not "alternatives to reality." Growing up "plugged in" and more tech-savvy than any previous generation, Millennials are better prepared and qualified to deal with both the positive developments and the challenges of the internet age, including, but not limited to trolling, Astro-turfing, and cyber warfare.

We've already seen Millennials start billion-dollar ventures and disrupt whole industries (Facebook and Snapchat), successfully serve in elected office (mayors Pete Buttigieg and Michael Tubbs), found non-profits and win a Nobel Peace Prize (Pakistani activist for female education, Malala Yousafzai). So, it's only a matter of time before we have our first Millennial Senator, President, and Supreme Court Justice. If that sounds scary to some reading this, don't worry, the sky is not falling. But, there are a number of fundamental realities we need to acknowledge if we're to all live on this Earth together (which we will get to shortly).

Too radical in their demands

This brings us to the final criticism: that Millennials are too radical, or just crazed followers of Bernie Sanders, a progressive and a socialist!

Conservative media and politicians like to pin labels on people who want to change this country for the better. They call them Liberals, Progressives, Socialists, Leftists, (and more) as if these terms were profanities. Once so defined, it's easy to dismiss both the people and the policies. But it's really just name calling, branding someone as "bad" and "un-American" without ever addressing what they actually stand for or have to say.

We believe in the progressive approach first articulated by our American Founders and Framers more than 200 years ago. Later, their ideas found expression in programs promulgated by the likes of Presidents Theodore Roosevelt, Franklin D. Roosevelt and Lyndon B. Johnson. The former created America's National Park system, helped build the Panama Canal, and made the first great attempt to break up certain predatory companies that used their power to monopolize and exploit American citizens. FDR expanded social programs to protect all Americans by initiating Social Security and disability payments for the blind or deaf. Johnson's efforts to usher in the Great Society were responsible for the greatest progressive shift by the federal government in American history by pursuing Equal Protection for all in civil and voting rights. Even President Harry Truman first proposed Universal Healthcare as part of his "Fair Deal" plan way back in 1949 while formally integrating the military.

That does not mean that Teddy Roosevelt, FDR, LBJ, or Truman were socialists or raving anti-capitalists. On the contrary, they followed the precepts of the founders of America, a system we call "Lockean" Capitalism.

First articulated by John Locke, an English philosopher who lived from 1632 to 1704, it refers to a form of capitalism that blends wealth building with the responsibility to share both the risks and benefits with all citizens, not just those that ruled society. In his seminal *Second Treatise of Civil Government*, written well before the American Revolution, Locke not only illustrated a utopian system of governance, but also one that would eventually and uniquely fit the new American economy and government as well. Instead of embracing the traditional roles of authoritative government typical of monarchies at the time, he argued that human beings were entitled to enjoy rights under a system of Natural Law that included certain rights to self-governance. Locke also carefully laid out a rationale for balancing the interests of individuals to create their own wealth independent of government, but also heavily reliant upon the mutual interests of the community.

The salient part of his treatise that caught the attention of our Founders and Framers was Locke's insistence that, although individuals may be free to acquire property and wealth, they could not flourish in isolation. He pushed the notion that safety and security provided by the community would be the best ends to protect the wealth and property of its members and the need to provide for "legitimate" democracy based upon the active political participation of all.

The Founding Fathers readily embraced this notion. In the Declaration of Independence, Thomas Jefferson used Locke's phrase "Life, Liberty and the pursuit of Property," altering it to read "Life, Liberty and the Pursuit of Happiness"—a clear intent to adopt Locke's view of capitalism working within a system of collective society enforcing norms, laws and common interests. The Founding Fathers and Framers recognized the necessity of combining capitalism with a heavy dose of society's sharing of risks and rewards.

Keep in mind that back in the day when a fire broke out, everyone ran to assist in putting it out, lest their own homes be burned if left unchecked. Publicly financed and operated fire brigades and police departments are the normal offshoot of this practice. As are the creation of highways and roads for the common good, public schools, the military to protect us; and the use of taxes to provide maintenance of roadways, hospitals, educational institutions and the like.

Although these notions have been embedded in America's foundation, they are often lost in the confusion about how the term Socialism is applied.

So, when members of the Right today slam the theory of Socialism for being un-American, they ignore the important role that collective sharing of risks and rewards had in the formation of our country. America was established using Locke's theories that no one can create wealth without some support from the community and, therefore, the individual also has a responsibility to support the stability and safety of the community in return.

As Progressive Lockean Capitalists, we believe that all American patriots should share that view, and Millennials can lead the way toward its general acceptance. In that spirit, let's look at what specific programs and issues rank high on the Millennial agenda.*

* Those who wish to get more involved with particular issues can also go to *www.BoomerstoMillennialstheBook.com*, where there are specific things to do for each of the sections discussed below.

I venture the challenging statement that if American democracy ceases to move forward as a living force, seeking day and night by peaceful means to better the lot of our citizens, fascism will grow in strength in our land.

—President Franklin D. Roosevelt

★★ PART II ★★

The Progressive Agenda
For Millennials

*My dream is of a place and a time
where America will once again be seen
as the last best hope of earth.*
—Abraham Lincoln

FOLLOW THE MONEY

Free Speech or Unbridled Corruption?

Money often costs too much.
—Ralph Waldo Emerson

During the 2010 State of the Union address, President Barack Obama criticized the Supreme Court's ruling regarding campaign finance in <u>Citizens United v. Federal Election Commission</u>. In response to his warning that the decision equating money with protected Free Speech would damage our electoral process, Supreme Court Justice Samuel Alito dissented. Captured on national television, he shook his head and mouthed the words, "Not true."

Except Obama was right and the Justice was wrong.

Money in politics. It's always been a problem, and it's always been used to maintain the status quo and existing power dynamics. During the final three decades of the 19th century, also known as the Gilded Age, America's ruling elite—robber barons like Andrew Carnegie, John Rockefeller, and John Jacob Astor—had judges and politicians in their pockets to do their bidding and promote their interest. We are living in another era in which wealthy Americans seek to buy influence in any way they can. It is estimated that in the elections since Citizens United just three wealthy men, the Koch Brothers, Charles and David, and Sheldon Adelson, have spent upwards of $1 billion on Super PACs and other political organizations. The Koch Brothers alone contributed over $889 Million themselves in the 2016 election cycle.[1]

Although the Left engages in campaign finance, what choice do its candidates have when facing the open pocket of those on the Right using the system? The Left openly seeks to limit campaign finance via legislation while the Right openly fights such efforts.

Giving large sums of money in secret to political action and interest groups allows donors to influence policies affecting all of us with impunity. In the process, they have managed to swing elections, install politicians up and down the ballot, and ultimately skew the balance of power to such a degree that Democrats need to win some elections by 5+ points just to earn equal representation.[2]

While political action and special interest groups are not allowed to formally coordinate with campaigns—the practice is illegal—there are few true barriers preventing candidates and their supporters from trying to circumvent campaign finance laws (Michael Cohen and Donald Trump are just the latest example of politicians flouting the law in an effort to win a campaign).

Another alarming example comes at the hands of one of the largest special interest groups in the country, the National Rifle Association. At the time of this writing, the NRA is under investigation for potentially conspiring with the Russian government and Russian oligarchs to funnel money into the 2016 Trump and GOP campaigns. Again, this was made possible by a Supreme Court that, for whatever reason, had faith in the fidelity of the campaign finance system. Money corrupts, and the majority on the Supreme Court, however Supreme they may be, seemingly made little to no effort to see this one coming.

An even more pernicious development of Citizens United is a tactic known as "astroturfing." The term describes organizations or groups with catchy names and large followings, yet people rarely realize that their supposed "grassroots" origins are a sham. Packaged to promote political goals tied to ideological groups, they are often opposed to the very interests and goals of the people they are attempting to influence. They are as fake as artificial grass, hence the name "astroturf." Perhaps the best known example was the Tea Party movement, which purported to be a populist uprising but was largely funded by Americans for Prosperity (AFP), a conservative political advocacy group founded by the billionaire Koch brothers.

Other examples include groups like "Working Families For Walmart," "Stop Too Big To Fail," and "Al Gore's Penguin Army," all of which were reactions to public outcries against corporations having too much control and paying their workers too little, or the inevitable climate crisis caused by fossil fuel corporations.[3] These groups all tried to bill themselves as grassroots, but it quickly became clear (due to their views and allegiances), that they were not interested in helping real people and were merely looking out for their own bottom-line.

These groups continue to influence the voting public while hiding behind the curtain of protections afforded by the Citizens United ruling.

Another consequence of the Citizens United ruling (perhaps unintended, perhaps not), was the role that money plays in candidates' "viability". Since the founding of our country, money has been a prerequisite for candidates vying for office. This is even more the case now. The sheer cost and time required to launch and run a campaign creates barriers for ordinary citizens and generally limits new candidates to the privileged few who have access to capital and can afford to take off from work for eight to 10 months during a campaign. Additionally, in recent cycles, both major political parties judge candidates by their ability to raise money or the size of their donor networks.

No wonder the U.S. Senate is the most powerful millionaire's club in the world and new candidates, by and large, are older, whiter, and skew male. We need to do a better job ensuring that our American elected officials actually look like America: ethnically diverse, middle-class, and as close to 50% proportionally female (if not more) as possible.

With income inequality at an all-time high and student loan debt totals reaching $1.5 trillion, the United States is creating a permanent underclass unable to participate in our democracy.[4] Republicans take pride in their ability to "create jobs," but if their jobs are mostly temporary, minimum-wage, or seasonal, we are only creating a system based on something akin to indentured servitude, where people have to go to work to buy the necessities, and there is no ability to save or get ahead. In an economy like this, the reality is that most of America won't have the right people representing them in Washington. Special interests and the wealthiest 1% will continue to call the shots and effectively bribe our elected officials into passing legislation that directly benefits them and hurts the rest of us. Ever hear of an effective lobbying group working for the poor? Neither have we.

In contrast to the current way of doing things, Millennials believe that everyone should have equal access to becoming a candidate for elected office. In recent years, a number of political organizations have started up dedicated to fighting back against money in politics. Perhaps the earliest and most prominent was Mayday PAC, a crowd-funded, non-partisan organization created by Harvard Law School professor and activist, Larry Lessig, whose purpose is to elect candidates to Congress who will overturn Citizens United. Other groups like Run For Something, She Should Run, Vote Run Lead, EMILY's List, Flippable and The Arena are recruiting, training, and supporting the campaigns of the next generation of leaders who are just everyday Americans tired of the status quo.

The 2016 presidential campaign of Bernie Sanders proved to the American public and aspiring politicians that instead of taking big money from a select few wealthy donors, candidates could raise the necessary funds by taking a little money from a large number of grassroots donors. In the wake of Sanders' success, instead of showcasing the total amount of money raised, candidates are beginning to showcase the number of individual donors that have given to their campaigns.

This is a game changer. As the electorate learns about the dangers of Corporate PAC money, more Democratic and progressive candidates will start to reject big, deep pocket, special interest, and corporate donors in favor building a wide network of grassroots donors. This approach will also become a routine requirement for endorsements—a way to prove allegiance to constituents and show commitment to their community. And when they win, they will be free from the burden of appeasing special interests (who are notoriously aggressive pushing their agenda).

The reemergence of "citizen politicians" willing to step up and become candidates themselves, without fear that only those with deep pockets can afford to run for office, is starting already. Many more grassroots candidates are beginning to run for office at all levels of government (local, state and national). Regardless of their success, this marks a turning point, the beginning of a positive future for our democracy. The roadblocks and barriers-to-entry need to come down, and there is no generation better positioned and prepared to make it happen than Millennials (with the support of non-Millennials). Here are a few basic electoral reforms that would increase voter participation and instill greater trust in our institutions: Automatic voter registration (automatically enrolling all eligible voters on their 18th birthday), ranked choice voting (allowing voters to select their candidate preferences in rank order, which reduces potential spoiler-effects of third-party candidates), and public matching of funds (instead of a campaign finance system where dark money flourishes). If we can create a more small "d" democratic system of elections, we will all win, because we will all be participating.

CLIMATE CHANGE

It's Getting Hot in Here

A nation that destroys its soils destroys itself.
Forests are the lungs of our land, purifying the air
and giving fresh strength to our people.

—President Franklin D. Roosevelt

In 2015, Senator James Inhofe, (R-OK) held up a snowball on the Senate floor to demonstrate that because water sometimes freezes in the form of snow, there couldn't be any sort of climate change.[5]

Since then, deniers have become less silly, yet just as bold faced and wrong. In the face of overwhelming scientific evidence, a significant number of conservative politicians and corporate apologists continue to insist climate change is a hoax.

The term "climate change" itself is a politically sanitized version of the original "global warming," which was weaponized by the Republican Party and its allies in the media. At its most extreme, it has been used to further attacks against environmental activism by portraying the warnings of the dire effects of climate change as a tactic to attack corporations and push "a socialist and globalist agenda upon America."[6]

Yet, the scientific evidence is indisputable. That's why you'll hear Republicans claim, "I'm not a scientist, but..." over and over again. They're pushing an agenda that is directly contrary to the science and evidence, and their cop-out position is that they're not scientists. Or they claim that "there is no scientific consensus," even though 97% of climate experts agree that man-made carbon emissions are directly contributing to climate change.

This refusal to accept scientific evidence is a common thread running through the Republican Know-Nothing Party of the modern era. Its game plan seems to be to shun the experts, go to the most ignorant practitioners, and then repeat their views back to its constituents. These climate change deniers are like the members of the Flat Earth Society, clutching at any straw to obfuscate the reality that our planet is round.

Why does the Pentagon take climate change seriously and run scenarios for dealing with rising oceans? Because the largest naval base in the world is located in Norfolk, Virginia, and it has its docks and access roads submerged and inaccessible by land during and after major storms. When they were constructed decades ago, no one anticipated that they would be too low by now.[7] In addition to the threats posed domestically, the impact of climate change will be felt worldwide, through drought, migration, famine, and other natural disasters.

This is not the place to debunk all of the nonsense spouted by deniers. Google "climate change denials" and you'll get plenty of information, both the hogwash and the real McCoy.

While politicians may argue and corporate interests may try their best to shield the truth, Millennials don't need rhetoric to appreciate that the environment is indeed changing as a direct result of man-made carbon emissions. They see it with their eyes every year: Summers are hotter, winters are more variable, storm systems are more powerful, and wildfires are more destructive. We must all come to face the facts: Climate change is real and affects all of us. This is not a political issue, it is a human issue.

Instead of politicizing climate change, Millennials must focus on the realities. While it may not be possible to convince the naysayers in the pockets of special interests and diehard deniers, there are both geographical and economic realities we all have to deal with. We may not be able to live entirely without carbon-based energy sources altogether right now, but existing technologies like wind and solar energy will begin to reverse the trend and if we act quickly enough, save our planet from the continued destructive use of fossil fuels.

At the same time, dealing with climate change offers vast economic opportunities for new energy industries which, tied to renewable energy sources, are both efficient and profitable. The case for innovation in energy is self-evident but, unless we act fast, the United States will fall behind China, India, and Europe in their bid to become the leaders of renewable energy.

For conservatives and capitalists, this should be the economic issue of the future. Studies show that alternative, green energy industries create jobs at a higher rate than coal and other fossil fuel industries.[8] If they really want to grow the economy and create strong, middle-class jobs, they should be championing wind and solar energy.

Over the past decades, the pressing issue of climate change has fallen into a political morass of misinformation, mockery and insult. Efforts to save our planet can be enhanced by showing money can be made, a free market can be sustained, religious obligations can be met, and our conscience can be clean by moving our economy towards renewable energy innovation.

It is not alarmist to argue that things need to be done quickly. Our polar icecaps are melting at a rapid pace, sea levels continue to rise, and cities like Miami are already experiencing flooding unheard of just 10 years ago.[9] If we fail to act now, we will lose the opportunity to be the global leader in renewable energy, and we may lose the opportunity to stave off potential disaster. Time is of the essence and remedial efforts to save our planet as we know it requires action, not further (and potentially fatal) delay.

EQUAL PROTECTION UNDER LAW

We The People Are All Equal

If someone tried to deprive you of your rights,
you've got to resist it. You've got to resent it.
You've got to fight against it.

—A. Philip Randolph

We all want safe and secure neighborhoods and communities, but there's no question, we have seen a blatant slide away from "To Serve and Protect" to one that protects the status quo.

The militarization of the police force with excess equipment from the Wars in Afghanistan and Iraq have led to what some describe as "occupying forces" in inner-city communities. This phenomenon is not unique to one community or state, and we've seen the backlash rise up in the forms of various groups decrying police brutality.

The Black Lives Matter movement, commonly known as BLM, came about as a result of police killing unarmed black men, often documented via cell phone footage, across the country. From Tamir Rice in Ohio, to Michael Brown in Ferguson, to Eric Garner in New York City, and all those whose names we don't know, the pattern is all-too-familiar. Police confront a brown or black man, often for a minor violation, but instead of calming things down, one (or both) parties escalate, and the police officers end up killing their suspect; becoming judge, jury, and executioner in public view.

What Millennials need to realize is that this isn't new. Some boomers have been fighting to right these wrongs for decades. In his "I Have a Dream" speech in Washington, D.C. in 1963, Dr. Martin Luther King said, "We can never be satisfied as long as the Negro is the victim of the unspeakable horrors of police brutality." The police brutality of 1963 is the same police brutality we are seeing now. Perhaps the only difference now is that technology has enabled the public to finally bear witness first hand to such flagrant discriminatory police behavior. The brutal beating of Rodney King by members of the Los Angeles Police Department (LAPD) in 1992 led to riots and a trial in which two of the four accused officers were found guilty. Was the act of police beating an unarmed black man reprehensible? Absolutely. But what was the reason that particular incident sparked such outrage? In all probability because it was captured by television cameras and broadcast for the world to see.

In the more recent cases of Michael Brown, Philando Castile, Eric Garner, Tamir Rice, and others, we see again that outrage followed because each of these incidents were recorded. They were captured on video by bystanders, body cameras, or dashboard cameras, and due to public outcry, the recordings were subsequently released on decentralized social media platforms. In Philando Castile's murder, his girlfriend went Live on Facebook, transmitting his daughter's crying in the back-seat of the car, the shots being fired, and her own incredulous, outraged response. Philando died shortly after. Although he was fired, the police officer who murdered him was acquitted of all charges at his trial.

Is it any wonder that black communities in America have little faith in the police force looking out for their interests? Yet, this problem is not limited to the African American community. Police, like any other group has its fair share of rogue elements. Race alone may not be the only factor in the abuses the public sustains. The traditional

"Blue Line" must be changed to hold all officers of the law accountable for any unlawful actions, regardless of the racial background of its abusers or victims.

Another reason for the distrust of law enforcement by many minorities and supporters of their rights has been the failed "War on Drugs." Cynically begun under Richard Nixon and expanded by Ronald Reagan and proponents of GOP "party first" policies, it was designed to root out and reduce crime but in the process it marginalized and incarcerated minorities in large numbers. Intended or not, the end result was that these communities were torn apart, removing any opportunity for normalcy in their homes. Additionally, because of felon disenfranchisement whereby criminals are stripped of their right to vote, many of their communities were neutralized as voting blocs.

This program has cost America millions of dollars and has placed more non-violent offenders in prisons in the United States than in any other country in the World.[10]

As a result of the failed War on Drugs, the "Home of the Free" currently does not include large swaths of American People of Color who have been deprived of freedom due to possession of drugs. Ironically, it has been shown time and time again that offenders with money are not treated the same as those without it. Mandatory Minimum sentencing was embraced by Conservatives as an effective crime solving tool, except it never reduced levels of crimes, but cynically shifted blocks of eligible voters into huge pools of ineligible voters who have been stripped of voting rights, all to ensure their political interests are shut out from the process.[11] The best example of this charade is the mandatory minimum criminal sentencing for crack cocaine versus powder cocaine. Less expensive crack cocaine, typically possessed by the urban poor, carry much stiffer minimum sentences than possession of powder cocaine (frequently more expensive and most likely possessed by affluent suburban whites).[12]

Democrats aren't free of blame either. In the 1990s, President Bill Clinton signed into law harsher crime bills in the hope of reducing crime. Spoiler alert: they didn't. Instead, more people ended up being locked up than before. As of 2018, there are more black and brown men incarcerated than at any point of the antebellum South when plantation owners held slaves.[13]

The negative costs of this "war" on drugs have been not only economic but social as well, resulting in the increased destruction of American families. When politicians point out the assault on the nuclear family, they fail to acknowledge how much the War on Drugs they designed and implemented has contributed to the breakup and fraying of the American social fabric.

The most immediate aspect of this faux war is the effect it has on community policing. Many citizens now view the police as enforcers tasked with controlling their behavior, enemies rather than trusted fellow human beings or friends to seek out for assistance when a crime is being committed. As a result, our police have become marginalized in the communities they are attempting to serve. But, instead of trying to repair the damage, politicians continue to project minorities as more dangerous to the rest of America's citizens. Instead of protecting everyone in our society, politicians expect police to protect only those that have leverage in the political process.

During the Trump administration, undocumented immigrants are afraid to call the police for fear they'll be referred to Immigration and Customs Enforcement (ICE), which will undoubtedly detain and deport them. This disincentive for our undocumented communities not only makes all of our communities less safe, it makes the police less safe. Instead of being clued into what's happening in the community, they're flying blind. It's a lose-lose scenario, but the Trump administration's focus is on terrorizing and scapegoating these communities despite their positive contributions, and regardless of whatever negative consequences might come of it, all for the cynical political points scored with its increasingly insecure base.

How can we combat it and reverse the trend? We can take notice of the state legislators around the country who are decriminalizing marijuana and exonerating nonviolent drug offenders, as well as the police departments and district attorneys who are taking steps back in the direction of fairer community policing.

There may be no better example of Criminal Justice reform than that of Larry Krasner, the newly elected District Attorney of Philadelphia who has been given a mandate to end mass incarceration in his city.

Tangible steps under Krasner's auspices include reforming the probation system, doing away with all marijuana charges as part of a prosecution, including paraphernalia charges, moving away from the common practice of opening plea deals with the maximum sentencing, and justifying to the judge and jury why the yearly cost of $42,000 to $60,000 per incarcerated person is necessary to rehabilitate that individual (and if it is not justifiable, then not sentencing that person to be incarcerated for that length of time).[14]

His fresh-thinking will take direct aim at harsh sentences and finding ways to reduce the burden not only on taxpayers, but also on the effects of those serving time. After all, when convicted felons serve their time, they will ultimately re-enter society. We want healthy citizens at all levels, and that includes fostering positive outcomes for those who have paid their debt to society in order to reduce the high rate of recidivism.

FIRST AMENDMENT

Free Speech and Religious Freedom

*Without freedom of thought, there can be
no such thing as wisdom—and no such thing
as public liberty without freedom of speech.*
—Benjamin Franklin

The First Amendment to the U. S. Constitution enshrined Free Speech as one of the most important principles of American Democracy. Few other countries in the world offer such a rigorous protection of people's right to speak their mind.

It is often said that Free Speech is not actually "free," however; that it comes at a great cost, both to protect it and to preserve it. But what cost do we pay when that speech is designed to inspire hatred and division in our nation? While some "free speech absolutists," may insist there is no just cause to curtail speech, of any kind, the right to speak has traditionally been limited in a number of ways. For example, we have a traditional common law basis for denying speech that is designed to defame individuals when there is no truth in it. That is why there are laws against slander and libel.

So why must we allow those people to have their say who use Free Speech to undermine our democracy? Recently, the United States Supreme Court has begun to use its conservative ideology in a way that has empowered something called "corporate rights." It has pursued the effort to use the First Amendment not only as a way to expand the reach of the First Amendment (to grant Corporations the right to ignore anti-discrimination regulations) but also to allow people to freely express their personal opinions when they are demonstrably false.

For example, the Supreme Court has ruled over the past decade that Corporations have First Amendment Free Speech Rights—so much so that if such a company disagrees with certain regulations it can refuse to post them because they have the right to regulate speech within their workspace. This has also been used by the Far Right to claim a religious basis for denying family planning and contraceptive insurance coverage to women working within their companies. Although on the surface it should make anyone scratch their heads as to how free speech could possibly be used to circumnavigate federal legislation, Conservatives have embraced this argument to limit individual liberties in a way the Framers could never have imagined or approved. These rulings fly in the face of "strict interpretations" of the Constitution and its former opposition to "activist" justices.

Although this sounds nutty, if one thinks it through based upon the logic of the Right, corporations, commonly known for centuries as "Legal Entities," now can control individual rights. And this is exactly what the Republican Party has been pursuing before the Courts. If a female employee seeks an abortion and her employer objects upon religious grounds, she may be terminated or denied equal access to health benefits. The Separation of Church and State continues to be viewed by the Right as a mere "inconvenience" or "misunderstanding" of the Framers' intent.

Another problem arising from the GOP's weaponizing of the First Amendment is the unfettered rise of "Fake News" in the broadcast and print media, and most prevalently via social media. Recently, Facebook admitted that it would not ban holocaust deniers from using its platform to spew hate and lies designed to confuse the public. Despite demonstrable facts that the holocaust was real, deniers have a far-reaching platform to corrode the truth and to muddy the waters with lies and distortions. The reason Facebook allows this to continue? The company claims it does not want to interfere with the rights of individuals to freely express their opinions, regardless of their motives.[15]

This goes a long way to explain why social media has become the generator of self-serving, opinion-based argument with a distaste for anyone that counters their opinions with actual facts. Knee-jerk reactions quickly come to the fore when opposition is raised under the guise that the "Fact Checkers need to be Fact Checked themselves."

One of the most egregious purveyors of lies and inflammatory rhetoric is Alex Jones and his online platform InfoWars, who consistently promotes lies and dangerous rhetoric. He has denied that the Sandy Hook school massacre happened and proclaimed he should "shoot Special Counsel Mueller." He quickly qualified the latter statement and then followed up by saying he meant it "only figuratively." But what if one of his followers takes it more seriously? We've already seen an example where an online conspiracy theory known as PizzaGate inspired a gunman to come to the rescue of children falsely imprisoned in a Hillary Clinton Sex Trafficking plot maintained in the basement of a Washington DC pizza joint, only to find the alarmed pizza owner shocked to be confronted by an armed gunman. There was no such scandal (the pizza parlor didn't even have a basement). Fortunately, no one was hurt in this lies-inspired attempt of vigilante justice.[16]

It is this misleading and outright deceptive speech that must be regulated or curtailed if it may "reasonably lead one to believe and then act...," which is the standard used in judicial proceedings. One that we can (and should) leverage when evaluating the consequences of unrestrained conspiracy theories intended to deceive, misinform, and undermine our democracy.

We can no longer operate at a crossroads here on our traditional "sides" of an argument. We as a society must turn the corner and at least engage in discussing the issue with the objective of finding a common-sense and Constitutional abiding solution to this very real problem.

Not only is this blatant deception dangerous to our society, it leads to the normalization of using "Alternative Facts" by our political leaders. Sure, we have all grown up with the understanding that used car salesmen and politicians will engage in "puffing" or embellishing facts in order to get a sale or a point across. But since the rise of the Republican Party's embrace of fake news, the practice has escalated and reached epidemic proportions. Donald Trump, the leader of the Republican Party, lies on an average of 7.6 times a day,[17] and few GOP members dare call him out.

America has never before experienced such bald-faced lying on the part of its elected leader. What would have been an easy target for ridicule is now embraced or condoned by the Right as a legitimate form of debate. Who would have thought that conservatives would support someone who follows the playbook of Joseph Goebbels, the Nazi minister of propaganda, who famously said, "If you repeat a lie often enough, people will believe it, and you will even come to believe it yourself."

When lies are used so brazenly to gain a political edge, one must wonder how much longer our democracy can exist. This is what Jefferson feared when he wrote about the "Fire bell in the Night!"—an alarm that rouses all citizens to act. How much longer will it take for Americans to realize we are living in dangerous times, different from dangerous times of the past?

Social media, hyper-partisan broadcast and print media, and the widespread support of political mayhem based upon prevarications is a fertile soil for Authoritarianism and Fascism. Freedom of Speech is one of the first rights to disappear under dictatorial regimes.

Boomers and Millennials alike must resist this enabling of lies and efforts to destroy our democratic institutions with all their might. We must characterize it for what it is: Unpatriotic, un-American, and heed this contemporary "Fire Bell in the Night" if we are to slow the steady movement towards Authoritarianism we are witnessing in real-time.

COMMON SENSE CONSTITUTIONAL GUN REFORM

What is Really Needed

*Cautious, careful people, always casting about
to preserve their reputations...can never effect a reform.*
—Susan B. Anthony

Millennials, perhaps more than any previous generation, have been in the actual firing line because of unresolved debates over how to guarantee citizens their rights to possess firearms while also protecting them from the use of guns in the public square.

As of this publication, 187,000 children have been exposed to gun violence at schools since the Columbine massacre in 1999.[18] Students nowadays are routinely subjected to active shooter drills. The potential for gun violence is treated like a fire, tornado, or some other natural event far beyond human control—go into lockdown mode, close the doors, bolt the windows, hide in the corner, and pray. Companies sell bulletproof book bags, students are taught how to use desks to shield themselves, and teachers are expected to protect and die for their students. It's a far cry from what school used to be.

Somehow during this period, politicians, with the financial and electoral support of the National Rifle Association (NRA), have cleverly maneuvered the electorate into actually ignoring the role firearms have in shootings.[19]

As recently as 2018, Betsy DeVos, Secretary of Education charged with reviewing gun violence after the massacre at Marjory Stoneman Douglas High School in Florida, which left 17 dead, formally appeared before Congress to state that all aspects of school violence are being reviewed and studied, but no review will be provided to look at the impact of firearms on gun related mass shootings. Yes, you read that right: *no review will be provided on the impact of firearms on gun related mass shootings.*[20] That's ignoring the most important part of the equation, like trying to understand the impact of boiling water on an egg without including the water, or the relation of red meat to heart disease without reviewing beef.

Since Parkland, there have been multiple school-related mass shootings. We are facing an epidemic of shootings in our schools, yet government officials in charge of protecting students throughout America turn a blind eye to the use of the weapons involved in the carnage.

How does such an important public policy matter get ignored? It can only be done when politicians expect the public to ignore realities as they relate to firearms. They must be reasonably regulated using common sense and Constitutional remedies.

Somehow, Millennials have also grown up in an era in which gun owners' Second Amendment Rights have seemingly been allowed to morph into the only Constitutional Right that matters. Gun owners have more rights to their weapons than citizens have a reasonable expectation to live in a safe society, free from potential death by firearms at any moment's notice.

When people raise the need for gun reform after a shooting, conservative politicians always say, "Now is not the right time to talk about this," only to wait until the news cycle passes and ignore the problem until the next massacre. The obvious answer to their shilly-shallying is

"If not now, when," and holding them accountable when they conveniently suffer from memory loss.

Another way they try to deflect legitimate conversations about possible solutions is to argue that a particular regulation—mandatory background checks, banning of bump stocks and assault weapons, for example—will not solve all gun violence. No one claimed that requiring people to wear seatbelts while driving their cars would eliminate all traffic deaths, yet that infringement on personal freedom does not raise public outrage. Instead, it has saved millions of lives.

The essential point to understand is that the problem of unchecked gun violence requires creative approaches that include sensible regulations, education, psychological treatment, and smart gun technology. Mandatory background checks, the closing of the private-gun sales loophole, and requiring finger-print or face-recognition technology to prevent anyone but the registered and licensed owner of a firearm from being able to shoot it, are just some examples of reforms that could be put into effect right now and save lives. Some may be incremental, but that is no reason to reject them outright. People understand that, which is why there is broad public appeal and support for a variety of solutions; what we are lacking is the political will on a federal level to achieve it.

Again, the most obvious policy solutions are to close the private-sale loophole and require anybody trying to purchase a firearm to undergo a background check. You'd think Republicans, who love the idea of waiting periods for women trying to have an abortion, would have no problem with that. Impulsive people don't need a firearm. After all, the Second Amendment of the Constitution calls for "a well-regulated militia" to wield deadly weapons—trained, checked, cleared, and responsible.

This is when conservatives and the NRA say, "It's not a gun problem, but a mental health problem." There is some truth to that argument, and providing more access to mental health care would be a good thing. But, while no country in the world is immune to mental health issues, only one country has a mass shooting problem that is not the result of terrorism, and it's not Sweden, Germany, England, Spain, China, Japan, Canada, or Australia. It's the United States of America.

When all else fails, gun advocates claim that any regulation of weaponry will create a dangerous, "slippery slope" that could lead to limiting the protection afforded in the Second Amendment. What these folks refuse to acknowledge is that there has never been an absolute right to possess firearms.

Since 1934, the manufacture, transfer and possession of a machine gun has been strictly regulated. To make this point, Federal law defines a machine gun as "any weapon which shoots, is designed to shoot, or can be readily restored to shoot, automatically more than one shot, without manual reloading, by a single function or trigger."[21]

So, why does the authority of Congress become non-existent whenever there is a demand for common-sense gun reform? Why the rhetoric that guns cannot be properly regulated? Because the gun lobby via the NRA and their affiliated supporters throughout the GOP and Right Wing media push a narrative that is inherently misleading and incorrect.

The issue of possessing hand guns was reviewed in 2008 by the Supreme Court in the matter of District of Columbia v. Heller. Justice Antonin Scalia writing for the majority affirmed the right to bear arms, but also noted that there are in fact limits on possessing guns. Scalia stated that the Constitution allows for the restriction against felons and the mentally ill from possessing a gun. Furthermore, guns can be prohibited from being carried in "sensitive areas" like schools and government offices. Justice Scalia also wrote, *"like most rights, the right secured by the Second Amendment is not unlimited. It is not a right to keep and carry a weapon whatsoever or in any manner wherefore and for whatever purpose."*

No more chilling words can be said to gun right supporters who claim that common sense gun reform is unconstitutional—the very case they use to make their argument includes the position that the rights under the Second Amendment are not "absolute." On actual legal grounds, the door remains open for legitimate and constitutional common-sense gun reform. Any argument against it ignores where the law currently stands, as articulated by the late strict constitutionalist and conservative hero, Justice Scalia.

These dubious arguments from conservatives are not lost on the next-generation. Millennials have grown up in a world where the lacking arguments of Second Amendment advocates have prevailed. Despite outcries when they occur, school shootings have become accepted as routine, almost a normal part of life. But they are not routine. Burying elementary, middle and high school students, teachers, classmates, and school guards is not normal.

Yes, other factors besides killing weapons may be at play, but every data-point says it's the guns. For 20 years, it's always been the guns.

Millennials may not end all mass shootings, but basic, common-sense gun regulation will go a long way toward achieving that goal.

WOMEN'S RIGHTS

It's About Time

*No country can ever truly flourish if it stifles
the potential of its women and deprives itself
of the contributions of half of its citizens.*
—Michelle Obama

The pursuit of equal rights for women is not a new phenomenon. Abigail Adams, one of our Founding Mothers made her feelings known often, not mincing words. In a March 1776 letter to her husband John while he was in Philadelphia attending the Second Continental Congress, she wrote, *"If particular care and attention is not paid to the ladies, we are determined to foment a rebellion, and will not hold ourselves bound by any laws in which we have no voice, or representation."* Her assertion was daring and prophetic.

Thousands of women since have taken to the streets, first to seek the right to vote and then for equal rights in all aspects of American life. Proposed as far back as 1921, progressive American women and their allies began a long journey to try to amend the Constitution by passing the Equal Rights Amendment (ERA). The amendment was designed to guarantee equal rights to all citizens, regardless of gender. While Conservatives argued that the Fourteenth Amendment already covers this area, activists asserted that until protections from gender discrimination are made explicit, women run the risk of being exposed to possible unwanted and unnecessary exploitation and discrimination. Unfortunately, the amendment failed to be ratified. A majority-male Congress passed legislation in 1972 to limit the time frame in which to ratify proposed Amendments to the Constitution to only seven years, in the wake of the ratification of the Twenty-Seventh Amendment, which took 203 years. It was a calculated, cynical ploy to derail the acceptance of the ERA. By the time the deadline expired, 35 states, three short of the required number, had ratified it.[22]

Now women must rely solely upon the interpretation of the Equal Protection Clause of the Fourteenth Amendment by the Supreme Court. Considering the election and confirmation of men alleged to have engaged in sexual assaults or paying off accusers to cover-up their true stories, women have a legitimate right to be angry and concerned about the future of their rights.

Shortly after President Trump's inauguration, the #MeToo movement boiled over. The outpouring of stories of sexual harassment, assault and abuse shocked the world and took down many powerful men whose history of exploitation was finally brought to light.

This reckoning has been a long time coming, and this is just the beginning. We clearly are undergoing a major cultural shift in attitude and expectations regarding women's rights. Sexual abuse and harassment disproportionately affects women and children. Recent studies indicate that nearly eight in 10 women will suffer some form of sexual harassment throughout their lives. Moreover, in many cases sexual abuse allegations continued to be downplayed, discouraging survivors from coming forward. When survivors do come forward, they frequently feel ashamed, and the alleged offenders are frequently given the benefit of the doubt. Given the traumatic effects and its widespread prevalence across all racial, ethnic, and socioeconomic groups, sexual abuse and harassment must be regarded as a non-partisan public health crisis.[23]

This is not the only area where women's rights continue to be under assault. Since the 1973 ruling of Roe v. Wade in which the Supreme Court codified into law a woman's right to an abortion at the federal level, religious and political conservatives in America have spent tens of millions of dollars and numerous election cycles trying to roll back the clock. Abortion has become an oppositional rallying cry for all those who believe that life begins at conception. While Republicans cannot outlaw abortion outright, they have achieved great legislative victories at the local and state level, specifically designed to limit women's access to safely terminate their pregnancies.

In some states, doctors are required by law to let patients know about potential complications, and in some cases, even tell their patients "facts" that are not backed by science.[24] This leads to a wrongful perpetuation of misinformation, something that most medical practitioners consider is antithetical to their practice.

Other laws require waiting periods for women interested in seeking abortions (forcing them to think even longer about a difficult and complicated personal decision). Still others establish regulations on the abortion clinic facilities compelling them the impossibly high standards of a state-of-the-art hospital (if they cannot meet the standards, they're forced to close down).

Where applicable, Republicans will do their best to cut any and all public funding for clinics as well. This is where the attacks on Planned Parenthood come into play, even though Planned Parenthood is the number one provider of medical services to women in the country (and only a small fraction of their budget is used for abortion services, and none of it from federal funds).[25]

In the minds of Republicans, limiting access to safe abortion is success. They want to go state by state and close down abortion providers. At the time of publication, there was only one clinic left in the entire state of Mississippi as a result of extreme, GOP-led legislature restrictions. The logical conclusion is simply that Republicans want to shut down all abortion clinics, and criminalize the act itself and the providers who engage in it. Granted, you can't trust anything that Donald Trump says, but on the campaign trail in 2016 he came out in favor of punishing women for having an abortion and the physicians who provide it.

In theory, these deterrent practices sound like it might actually reduce the number of abortions, but this couldn't be further from the truth. It simply reduces the number of safe abortions available to women. Further, it ensures that abortion becomes an issue of social and racial justice. In areas where abortion clinics have been limited, those with the means and resources will simply travel to a neighboring state to have an abortion. In general, this restricts the number of women who end up having abortions to an older, whiter, and richer population.

Even though others may not be able to afford abortions, this doesn't mean that they won't be getting them. What is critical to note is that, while Republicans are doing their best to ban abortion on local, state, and federal levels, it is simply impossible to ban abortions entirely. What they will end up achieving, if successful, is banning access to *safe* abortion, indifferent to the immense toll on womens' mental and physical health.

Prior to Roe v. Wade, women underwent risky abortion procedures even though it was against the law. An unwanted pregnancy is an unwanted pregnancy, and a determined person will find a way to not carry the fetus to term. Mounting outrage over stories of back alley abortions, in some cases fatal for the mother, and botched procedures by hack physicians operating illegally, were one of the reasons for Roe v. Wade. Our solution shouldn't be to outlaw the practice, it should be to ensure that they are able to do so in a healthy and safe environment without jeopardizing their life.

There are also proven ways to reduce abortions that don't include criminalizing women. It all starts with education. If Republicans actually wanted to reduce abortions, they'd get rid of abstinence-only sex education in schools and expand access to contraceptives. Fewer teenagers would be having unprotected sex, and in turn, fewer women would have unwanted pregnancies. Instead, in much of the country, sex education is a taboo topic (going back to America's puritan and religious beliefs), and teenagers aren't being properly taught about their sexual health and habits. This leads them to engage in risky sexual acts, and the result is unwanted pregnancies.

Also frequently lost in the debate about abortion is that women cannot spontaneously become pregnant on their own. If Republicans really wanted to hold people accountable for abortion and unwanted pregnancies, they would need to take into consideration the men who impregnated women in the first place. But this isn't a part of their concern. Instead, they're hyper-focused on ensuring women carry to term as many babies as they can. They want to legislate rules and regulations regarding women's bodies (while claiming to be the party of "small government"). It's another example of Republicans and religious conservatives trying to impose their belief system on others. They do not agree that, while we have freedom of religion in this country, we also have freedom *from* religion.

There is also considerable hypocrisy on the Right when it comes to safeguarding one's privacy. While the Republicans argue time and again about preserving personal freedom and limiting government interference, they don't seem to be concerned about either when it comes to regulating and potentially outlawing women's abortion rights.

Ultimately, for Millennials this argument comes down to the basic human right of maintaining bodily autonomy. Most would agree that forcing someone into slavery is wrong. The same is the case with forcing someone to do something with their body that they do not want to do. The same principle should apply to both. A woman's right to determine her reproductive decisions should not be open for public debate.

As men, we've never been in the position of having to choose between carrying a pregnancy to term or not, and we never will be. But, can you imagine if men were able to get pregnant? Can you imagine men making the argument to other men they cannot decide what they're able to do with their own bodies? It would never happen.

So, why should we tolerate this argument towards women? The data show that Millennials overwhelmingly believe in a woman's right to choose. They have witnessed first-hand the hypocrisy of Republicans claiming to be pro-life while cutting social services for the poor. In reality, Republicans are simply pro-birth and show little interest in feeding, clothing, educating, or providing healthcare for that child once it's born.

As progressives, we need to do a better job ensuring that everyone is able to realize basic human rights. For women, the pursuit of Life, Liberty, and Happiness must start with having bodily autonomy and the right to say when and where a pregnancy starts, and when and where a pregnancy ends.

LGBTQ+

Why They Must Be Protected

*All young people, regardless of sexual orientation or
identity, deserve a safe and supportive environment
in which to achieve their full potential.*
—Harvey Milk

While largely pushed into the shadows or shunned into "the closet" for most of America's history, the American LGBTQ+ community has always existed, and is as American as apple pie.

According to many historians, the first well-known LGBTQ+ American was Friedrich Wilhelm Von Steuben, better known as Baron Von Steuben, who rose to prominence during the Revolutionary War. While it was never confirmed, most historians agree that Von Steuben left Germany under suspicion of homosexuality, and arrived in the United States with his reputation soon to follow.

These rumors and accusations didn't stop General George Washington from hiring him and placing him in a leadership role in the Continental Army (after all, he had a war to win). Von Steuben served as George Washington's Chief of Staff and Inspector General of the Continental Army, and ultimately rose to the rank of Major General. He authored *Regulations for the Order and Discipline of the Troops of the United States*, which became the premiere document for training the

Continental Army, and functioned as the single most used drill manual until the War of 1812. After the Revolutionary War, Congress honored Von Steuben for his service and granted him a full military pension.

All of this to say, if it weren't for the contributions of a member of the LGBTQ+ community, the Continental Army wouldn't have been trained as well and the course of the Revolutionary War, as well as the outcome, might have been very different.

Yet, at the time in Colonial America and for the next 200 years, homosexuality was criminalized. Because of the Puritan and religious beliefs commonly held in the colonies, "sodomy" and "buggery" were treated as capital offenses, met with penalties of expulsion from the community or death in some areas. It was a felony to be caught cross-dressing in public.

The legacy of these beliefs and laws remains to this day in the Religious Right's assault on civil liberties. And even extending beyond Evangelical Christians beliefs towards the LGBTQ+ community, these same provincial attitudes towards the LGBTQ+ community are common in more rural and conservative areas, leading to widespread misunderstanding of the issues and sharply prejudiced attitudes.

Although there have been considerable advancements in the fight for equality for all minorities, we are far from finished. In over two-dozen states, people can be fired from their job, discriminated against in the workplace, refused housing, medical care, or other services simply because they are LGBTQ+.[26] While conservatives make the argument that this is a matter of "equal protection under the law" and an issue concerning the Fourteenth Amendment, there are no explicit protections for this community, and we've seen that there definitely need to be.

Lately, the members of the Religious Right have pushed for laws asserting their "freedom of religion" and the right to practice their religion as they please. Supreme Court decisions such as <u>Burwell v. Hobby Lobby</u> have effectively inscribed into law the right to discriminate under the guise of religious liberty.[27] Combine judicial rulings with the dehumanizing rhetoric of hate coming from the Right, and you have a dangerous, volatile environment.

Violence against the LGBTQ+ community is not new. We only need to go back to the police raids on gay bars common in the 1950s and 1960s to see evidence of institutional violence perpetrated against the most marginalized in our society.

Following one of these raids on a gay bar in Manhattan, the LGBTQ+ community pushed-back publicly and violently. The Stonewall Riots, widely understood as one of the most important moments in the Gay Rights movement, brought the LGBTQ+ community into the public spotlight and told the world it existed, was here to stay, and would no longer tolerate systemic aggression against its members.

Over the course of the next two decades, as a result of intense political organizing, numerous states took legislative action to decriminalize consensual same-sex sexual acts, but the fight for equality was just getting started.

It wasn't until the AIDS crisis affected straight men and women that the American public and its political leaders took note. In the meantime, members of the LGBTQ+ community were dying by the tens of thousands. Larry Kramer, the founder of Gay Men's Health Crisis witnessed his friends become ill and die as a result of AIDS, and it wasn't until he organized large public civil disobedience campaigns through his organization ACT UP that he was able to secure the attention of those in power. It took disruption of the status quo to make a statement and be heard, and the results of his civil disobedience campaign led to the dedication of substantial funds to tackle the AIDS epidemic in the United States (where more than 600,000 people died).[28]

Turning a blind eye to a developing crisis wasn't just a matter of homophobia and fear of "the other." It was political cowardice and an inability to have human-centered and constituent-centered principles and values guiding the decisions of elected officials. If they had the moral courage to focus on the issue that mattered, saving the lives of their constituents, it wouldn't have entered their mind that these people were gay, straight, white, black, or other. Instead, they would have simply viewed them as people in need of help. But because they made decisions based on fear and prejudice, the crisis was prolonged in ways that costs thousands of lives. We can, and should, learn from their mistakes.

Similar prejudiced attitudes contributed to the long-delay of politicians publicly supporting same-sex marriage, even though a majority of the American public was in favor. Barack Obama was "still evolving" on the issue in 2010, and it took his vice president, Joe Biden, to prod him into action two years later.[29] Obama was often falsely accused of "leading from behind," but in this case the charge was true. Hillary Clinton didn't publicly endorse the idea of same-sex marriage until 2013.

Millennials, having come of age in a post-AIDS crisis world where popular culture featured many LGBTQ+ characters in television sitcoms and dramas, and as hosts of talk-shows, generally are more supportive of the LGBTQ+ community.

But the issue of leadership remains. What we want in the coming years are activist-leaders: people who aren't afraid to stand out front and shape public opinion in the progressive direction it needs to go, instead of reacting and molding their views to that of the broader electorate.

If that means active protest, so be it. The tactics used by the pioneers at Stonewall, and by Larry Kramer and ACT UP, were those of civil disobedience. This is core to making progressive change and reshaping public opinion and attitudes. We saw it in the Civil Rights movement, in the protests against the Vietnam War, in the fight for marriage equality, and now we're seeing it with the Women's March, the Climate March, and the Abolish ICE movement.

Protest is meant to be public and disruptive. If it didn't disrupt, it wouldn't capture the attention of the country, and it ultimately would not be successful. We must continue our tradition of civil disobedience and we should do it with a strong moral core and a moral code that necessitates focusing on the most marginalized.

STUDENT LOANS

Too Much Financial Stress

The need for a college education is even more important now than it was before, but I think that the increased costs are a very severe obstacle to access. It is an American dream, and I think that one of our challenges is to find a way to make that available.

—Roy Romer

During the westward expansion of the United States, settlers braved all kinds of dangers in order to start a new life. When they established small towns and villages on the prairies, in the mountains, and then along the Pacific Coast, they used three ways to build community—religion, law and education. They brought in a preacher to lead their congregation, appointed a sheriff to keep the peace, and hired a school teacher to establish and run the local, one-room schoolhouse.

Education has always been a hallmark of America. This notion goes back all the way to our Founders and Framers, who maintained from the outset that Democracy requires an educated public.

Yet today, various segments of society have been led to believe that those with higher levels of education along with their prosperity have somehow put themselves "above" the rest of "ordinary Americans." As a result, "elitism" has been sold to many as a divisive term, one that connotes superiority of the few over the many. For decades, in a continuous effort to divide American society, the conservative media has been associating "elitism" as a negative to be avoided—all in a continuous effort to divide our society. Hypocritically, the Right often seems to vilify the Left as being out of touch with the average American while embracing its own view that America is only great when those with great wealth lead our nation.

This was evident with its embrace of Donald Trump the candidate as someone who could bring his vast business acumen to the White House, when in reality, Trump brought few qualities necessary to be an effective president. Instead of embracing the highly educated and "specialists" in their particular fields—medicine, law, education, finance, etc.—Conservatives portray elites as something to be feared or mistrusted. How this "disconnect" has worked for them simply illustrates how tribal our nation has actually become—pitting Americans against Americans. Education is not something to be dismissed as unnecessary as it has always been a hallmark of American democracy.

Investing in our children and our future is one of the pillars of our success. Our immigrant parents and grandparents left countries that barred them from access to higher education. Many encouraged their children and grandchildren to be the first to obtain a college degree.

And with Millennials, those investments have paid off. Millennials are the most educated, most technologically-literate generation in history. The reason: by the time Boomers came along, many of their fathers, having fought in World War II, benefited from opportunities like the GI Bill. Even during this time of great prosperity and significant growth in the middle-class, not everyone benefited from the policies at the time. Racist rules like "red-lining," made explicit as part of the GI Bill and subsequent acts, prevented black veterans from receiving the same loans, mortgages, and opportunities as their white counterparts.[30] As time went on and wealth transferred hands from one generation to the next, increasingly the cycle of intergenerational poverty spread to ever larger sections of Americans, while smaller groups were able to prosper.

Generally, a rising tide lifts all boats. And this philosophy worked for a long time. Progressive programs like Bright Futures in Florida, for example, which allows high achievers to attend state universities tuition-free, have helped students regardless of their financial backgrounds, and these were good, solid programs that helped students begin their future on the right foot.

For a while, public college and university systems in all 50 States offered affordable education, contributing to upward mobility and swelling the ranks of the middle class. But over the last several decades, our country has retreated from this valuable approach. Education has become a political issue, used as a partisan football to kick around and to attract voters with mostly empty promises. Millennials well remember the hoopla surrounding "No Child Left Behind" during the second Bush presidency, which was announced with great fanfares and accomplished little.

In recent years as the education debates have become more ideological, conservatives have started to argue that taxpayers' money is being "wasted" on public education. The alternatives they offer—vouchers, charter schools, privatizing schools—have done little to improve education across the board.[31] The result, whether intended or not, is to create a two-tiered system in which the wealthy and privileged will have easy access to the best schools, while the rest, and poor people in particular, will languish in perpetually underfunded educational institutions.

This is not only reprehensible, but short-sighted as well. Our human capital, our people, are the most important asset we have. That's why we were able to win World War II and the space race, create the internet, and build the most sophisticated economy on the planet. Was it a liberal notion to fly to the moon? Absolutely! And the advances in technology from the "space race" are still enjoyed by millions today. Generally speaking, high school dropouts did not contribute towards these advances; those with higher education did.

Millennials are not confused by the attacks on "elites" and the efforts to gut our public school system. They value education as much as their forebears, and they understand the benefits of a college degree.

Yet one thing stands in the way of higher education paying off for everyone: the incredibly high cost of attaining higher education. From trade schools to universities, the latest data indicate that student loan debt in 2018 exceeds $1.5 trillion.[32]

College tuition costs, even at public State schools, have risen astronomically. The cost of higher education has outpaced even skyrocketing healthcare costs. The consumer price index since 1982 has risen 115% while the cost of higher education has risen almost 500%.[33]

While earning a college diploma continues to be touted as a prerequisite for career success and higher earnings in the job market, obtaining it has become so expensive that many can't afford it or have to take out enormous loans, saddling their future with heavy debt.

Hundreds of millions of dollars paid monthly in loan interest and principal leaves Millennials' bank accounts. That money is not feeding back into the economy. It's going into the pockets of private student loan lenders who engage in predatory lending activities. Imagine how much more the economy would be humming if recent graduates could buy a car, or save a down payment for a house, instead of handing off the lion's share of their disposable income to student loan providers?

The economic weight of student loan debt has a detrimental effect on the psyche of the young students and the actual economy as well. Money spent on student loan interest charged at rates far higher than those levied on mortgages or consumer credit illustrates how unfair the cost of obtaining student loans has become.

Just about every college graduate struggling under the weight of student loan debt is forced to pay student loans first before considering marriage, having a family, buying a home, purchasing furnishings for said home, buying an automobile, etc. Instead of pumping money into the economy on a daily basis, young Americans are strapped with stifling loan repayments, so large they cannot afford to start out in America as their parents and grandparents did. It is one thing to start with nothing, it's another to be forced into living with nothing until student debts are repaid.

Further, there are laws in place making it impossible for graduates to be relieved of their student loan debt through bankruptcy. Ironically, businesses and individuals have access to financial debt relief for a variety of debts, but not for student loans. In some instances, even death will not relieve the borrower (and co-signer) of relief. If a student dies, his or her loans could potentially transfer to someone else. But if that student were just another company that failed, like Donald Trump's six businesses, he or she could take out loans and then declare bankruptcy over and over again, and never lose any personal assets.

The double-standard is astounding and inexcusable. Why is the American government forcing Americans to decide if higher education is worth the financial costs? The end result is that we all lose out on the benefits of having an educated public.

How can we expect as a nation to foster progress when Millennials are forced to drown under the pressure of education debt? This is a national problem that demands attention and relief from our political leaders. Education was never intended to be a "Profit Center" for our government and/or banks. Yet, given the current political climate, this problem will continue to fester without remedy unless Millennials and a new crop of elected officials address it, going against the prevailing tide.

Just providing debt relief is not enough, however. We must reverse the trend and invest more in public education again. What you learn shouldn't be dependent on what zip code you live in and how high the property taxes are in your school district. We need to ensure equal access to education and opportunities. It sounds simple, but when we are all doing better and are more educated, society, as a collective, will do better as well.

NEWS AND SOCIAL MEDIA

Your Facts or Mine?

*I think it is absolutely essential in a democracy
to have competition in the media, a lot of competition,
and we seem to be moving away from that.*

—Walter Cronkite

In 1974 Carl Bernstein and Bob Woodward published *All the President's Men*, their gripping account of how they uncovered the Watergate scandal which, ultimately led to President Nixon's resignation. The movie version that came out two years later, starring Dustin Hoffman and Robert Redford, turned them into heroes. For years after, journalism majors dreamed of becoming investigative reporters and following in their footsteps.

In recent decades, however, with the marginalization of print media, and the rise of punditry and infotainment, solid journalism and good, honest reporting has become increasingly rare. As a result, we have seen considerable degradation of our news media. If you ever wondered why we have become a nation that no longer uses our critical thinking skills, just look at the rise of the non-expert infotainment stars—from Rush Limbaugh, Glenn Beck, Sean Hannity, Tucker Carlson and Alex Jones. At the same time, social media have made experts of know-nothings, who spread their opinions framed as expertise via Facebook, Twitter and Instagram.

During a hurricane, suddenly everybody is a hurricane expert; during a Supreme Court ruling, SCOTUS experts come out of the woodwork. Name the topic or occasion, and people are eager to make their voices heard weighing in with passion and force. Whether or not they are well-informed or simply spouting run-of-the-mill opinions heard from their fiends or neighbors, social media gives them a forum and level playing field. Modern media activity is less about consuming, and more about producing. In a world where everyone is a content creator, and everyone thinks he or she has an audience, no one wants to listen. Instead, people want to hear themselves talk, and actively look through the increasing number of likes, comments, and shares as evidence that they're being listened to.

Although news media has always been expected to make a profit, money wasn't the bottom line. The television companies made their money on actual entertainment—advertising on sitcoms, dramas and sporting events. It was generally understood that, as users of the bandwidth granted to them by the Federal Communications Commision (FCC), they owed the public honest news broadcasting. Instead of being a 24-hour source of infotainment, actual network news ran no more than 30 minutes in length and featured the most newsworthy stories of the day. It also covered more world news related content. Americans used to know news broadcasts were developed, produced and aired with integrity and honesty by reporters from news bureaus located across the globe.

That is no longer the case. With the rise of cable and wall-to-wall coverage, news channels operate like all other forms of business and as such, no longer act in their role of the Fourth Estate, the Free Press guaranteed by the Constitution to bring the public actual, fact-based news and related information. Instead media must chase revenue and profits like any other corporation. This has led to a reduction in actual newsgathering in favor of fancy bells and whistles—graphics, soundtracks and iconic "Breaking News" logos—in order to stir up viewers with manufactured drama so that more of the public will tune in. The more people watch, the more advertising money the stations make.

Talking heads from both sides of the aisle engage in noisy, vocal, and sometimes staged disagreements to gin up the emotions of viewers. Remember the empty podium shots during the 2016 campaign when cable news stations spent seemingly endless periods of time awaiting Donald Trump's arrival at rallies? Meanwhile, Hillary Clinton received only a fraction of the live coverage, and the majority of time spent discussing her campaign had a negative tone, usually regarding her emails.

Exacerbating the problem of biased coverage has been the FCC allowing news gathering and reporting organizations to consolidate ownership. We no longer enjoy independent news outlets and instead face a barrage of monopoly-owned, corporate-directed, produced and scripted news. In hundreds of local markets, it is now commonplace to have opinion tinged reporting broadcast—often with identical phrases and talking points—all presenting a homogenized and massaged message designed to steer audiences into one political camp or another.[34] Gone are the days of large scale independent journalism. Corporate Journalism has taken over and the resulting dangers to our democracy are obvious.

With the never-ending expansion of social media, we are witnessing the "dumbing down of America" at a pace not seen before in our collective history. Social media can be a vital mechanism to exchange new ideas and to communicate solidarity on policy issues. Yet, it has also become the bastion of misdirection, misleading and outright deception, manipulating the electorate via paid ads with falsehoods and lies. Because these companies operate in a capitalistic economy and trade in the public markets, they have no incentive to stop accepting political advertisement dollars. Their sole desire is to maximize profits, return value to their shareholders, and maintain a platform with high growth and engagement. To executives at Twitter, a white supremacist engaging and organizing via tweets is just as good in their mind as a Civil Rights group using the service. In fact, both doing it is the best scenario. The more people actively engaging on the platform, the better Facebook and Twitter do as a company.

Taking this one step further, all you need to do is look at the 2016 election. Facebook ran political ads after accepting Russian rubles in payment for them. Not only is such practice against Campaign Finance Law (no foreign actor shall engage in political activity of any kind), Facebook happily profited from the transaction.

Mark Zuckerberg himself has said that he doesn't believe Facebook has an obligation to censor content one way or another. Which makes sense, because why would Facebook kick off a user who's paying them money to run ads in exactly the way the platform was designed to be utilized? Facebook and Twitter's obsession with "neutrality" in the face of disgusting abuse is a feature, not a bug. It was designed to encourage engagement and remain as addicting for consumers (and profitable for them) as possible.

This is not to say, however, that governments are not taking notice. These companies were called to testify to both Congress and the UK Parliament following the 2016 election, and the European Union has recently begun implementing the far-reaching General Data Protection Regulation (GDPR) as a means of protecting user privacy.[35] How successful this act will end up being, or how long until it becomes obsolete, remains to be seen.

Until these companies are regulated, they will have no incentive to curb their practices and stop accepting political advertising dollars, regardless of intent and origin.

Any cursory view of Facebook, Twitter, Instagram and hyper-partisan blogs and ideological websites will reveal how easy it is to use the Internet to flood society with both honest and dishonest postings. In recent years, the public has been so inundated with misdirection, misinformation and deception that Fake News ("Alternative Facts") threatens to overwhelm fact-based reality. When President Trump retweets false claims he read on some Right Wing website or heard on Fox Morning News, such as "large scale killing of farmers" in South Africa, imbuing the assertion with the semblance of truth, it becomes clear how easy it is to generate believable lies.[36]

Such believable lies permeate the social media universe, and before you know it, they're regular talking points of each respective camp. As an electorate, we need to be more aware of the incoming threats posed by our newly connected world.

Generally speaking, Millennials are more aware of potential cybersecurity threats than previous generations, having grown up in a digital-first world and the threat of downloading a computer worm or virus to their PCs, Macbooks, smartphones, or tablets. But when it comes to privacy concerns, an interesting paradox emerges. Various studies have indicated that Millennials who have, after all, voluntarily disclosed a great deal of their personal lives online via social media and the apps that they download, are comfortable with businesses collecting and leveraging their data to better tailor products to them. That may be changing, however. More recent studies, including one from Gallup in 2016, suggest that Millennials are growing skeptical of social media sites tapping their personal data for commercial usage.[37]

Ever since Ronald Reagan called for the end of the Fairness Doctrine, political advertising money has been flooding into the Infotainment channels, pushing talking points and narratives disguised as news. This must end. Media must be required to produce accurate news and information. In the event they continue the path of providing fiction-based Infotainment, then they must identify throughout the broadcast(s) they are an entertainment network only not to be confused with real fact-based news outlet.

And for those who think this sounds radical, again, this isn't uncommon in other countries. Canada and the United Kingdom don't have Fox News, and surprise, surprise, they have significantly less conspiracy-theory spouting politicians.

CYBERSECURITY AND PRIVACY

Whose Business Is It Anyway?

The potential for the abuse of power through digital networks—upon which we the people now depend for nearly everything, including our politics—is one of the most insidious threats to democracy in the Internet age.

—Rebecca MacKinnon

Since the passage of the Patriot Act (enacted shortly after 9/11), the country has seen an expansion of governmental rights to collect personal data on every American. From accessing virtually anything via the Internet (Emails, Instant Messages, Facebook posts, Tweets, online purchases to any credit transactions, and more), Americans are now an open book for companies to collect and analyze our data. Millennials know this first hand, as their interaction with technology has been intimate since the early days of AOL Dial-Up and the original GameBoy.

From facial recognition and touch ID fingerprint recognition to instant internet advertisements based upon stored purchasing histories, Millennials know the future of cybersecurity is a very real concern. Perhaps more dangerous than the wholesale collection of personal data is the threat of using that data to manipulate citizens, or even impersonate them. Consider how easy it is to photoshop images. Now imagine how in the near future, a type of photoshopping, or video or audio editing will enable everyday people to take your words and images and alter them to create a totally different take. There are already "Bad Lip Reading" videos circulating the internet, but imagine this is used in a malicious attempt to incite violence. Politicians and law enforcement could easily use these altered images or videos to proceed with enforcing police actions without actual probable cause other than the "doctored" photo or speech. Would Americans be able to discern whether or not the next President or foreign leader "actually" said what appears in those videos or audio clips? In the future, there may come a time where it is impossible to distinguish between what is real and what is fake, and that should worry every American.

Since the advent of the Internet, there has been a seismic shift in how people view their rights to privacy. For Baby Boomers, privacy was something held to be very dear. In fact, due to many Boomers protesting the Vietnam War, they witnessed first-hand the public disclosure of the unlawful expansion by a corrupt Nixon White House's use of criminal investigative mechanisms to spy on any American via the FBI's COINTELPRO program.[38]

As a result, although Boomers lacked a level of "tech-savviness", they appreciated the need to keep personal information safeguarded from potential governmental intrusion. Granted, Boomers at the time did not have access to high speed computers (the computing power of sending and landing man on the moon is now overpowered by the computing power of the average cell phone). Without cell phones or the Internet, it is impossible to compare Boomers' positions of protecting privacy with those facing Millennials, however, it is safe to claim that Boomers generally respected the right to keep personal information private.

Today, more and more information is collected without anyone's active knowledge. Data once considered private is now routinely collated from everything relating to personal shopping habits to medical treatments. Banking information is available online and currently, cyber-crimes are moving to the forefront as even basic assemblers of personal information make it readily available to others by offering to sell it or negligently allowing it to be stolen through cybertheft. This became evident with the exposure of Cambridge Analytica and its role in providing personal data from social media sites like Facebook and Twitter in an effort to manipulate the electorate shortly before the 2016 elections.

Boomer politicians are to blame for ignoring the threats to our personal privacy by failing to understand and appreciate the mechanisms of the Internet and the dangers it inherently possesses. Since the onset of the Internet, Boomers have maintained a sort of naïve "innocence" when it comes to technological advancements. As a result, far too often Boomers have relied on our elected leadership to be vested in understanding the new electronic information age—yet these very same leaders carry the same naïve ignorance when it comes to the internet. This naivety has been clearly illustrated by members of Congress who clearly have no idea how our new cyber era actually works.[39]

As a result, Boomers generally have abdicated leadership when it comes to protecting citizens from cyber-crime. Millennials on the other hand, not only appreciate the positives and negatives of our newly connected world, they also understand more broadly how actual program coding works and what steps will need to be made in the near future to protect us all from ever-growing cyber-crime schemes. From "phishing" to identity theft, to hacking and "skimming" credit cards and banking information, to breaking into our nation's national security apparatus, Millennials are far better equipped to lead us towards a more secure online landscape.

SOCIAL SECURITY AND MEDICARE

Entitlements or Contract Rights?

*Should any political party attempt to abolish social
security, unemployment insurance, and eliminate
labor laws and farm programs, you would not hear
of that party again in our political history.*
—Dwight D. Eisenhower

Before Social Security was first introduced nation-wide, a number
of states were already experimenting with providing a foundation of
financial support for their elderly population. During the Great Depression, millions of Americans lost their savings as well as their jobs
and the first sizeable group to call on the Federal government to step in
was the "Bonus Army," a group of activist veterans who had fought in
World War I. They descended on Washington in 1932 and demanded
an advance of their military pensions. While setting up tent camps, dis-
paraged in the press as "Hoovervilles," the veterans failed to persuade
Congress and President Herbert Hoover to grant their demands. On
the latter's orders, then Army Chief of Staff, General Douglas MacAr-
thur, lined up military units and forcibly evicted the protesters. Images of the U.S. Army burning the shantytown to the ground were
published in virtually every newspaper throughout the land, leading
to an outpouring of sympathy for the veterans and their dire need for
immediate financial assistance.[40]

While Governor of the State of New York, Franklin D. Roosevelt had signed into law one of the first public welfare assistance programs in the country. After his first inauguration as president, he initiated a review of "Old Age and Survivors" benefits. As a result, in 1935 the Social Security Board was created to administer a new program and to explain to Americans why paying into its fund would provide basic financial support after retirement. Because of his own experience with polio, FDR understood the financial needs of the disabled and by 1939 the program included payments to Americans that were deaf and/or blind. By 1946, the Social Security Administration took over the reins of the program.[41]

It has been said that Millennials will be the first generation of Americans to live a life fundamentally different than that experienced by Baby Boomers. Boomers as infants enjoyed the post-war boon of the 1950's and grew up watching the expansion of the use of free speech and assembly during the Vietnam War. Boomers also enjoyed a renewed sense of optimism in our government and the media witnessing the coverage of the corruption of the Nixon White House and have benefited from the explosion in new technologies that improve our daily lives.

But Boomers also found education and housing costs to be somewhat affordable and traditionally worked jobs that became their careers, staying with one employer and entitling them to receive a form of defined benefit plan in the form of a pension. Today, Millennials generally can expect to change their jobs at least 15 to 20 times in their working lives. Fewer and fewer Millennials also possess a job that provides any pension benefits.[42]

With all of the talk of Social Security and Medicare running out of money (since the government routinely "borrows" heavily from the Social Security Trust Fund), Millennials are left with the empty feeling that they will be paying for the Social Security and Medicare coverage of Boomers without any real expectation of enjoying the benefits themselves. According to the Social Security Office of Retirement and Disability Policy, the programs will be running a shortfall in funding by 2035.[43] Although Boomers know this is inherently unfair to Millennials, their collective inaction on this front seems to reflect an opinion of "I got mine" with less and less concern for Millennials and how the social safety nets of Social Security and Medicare will be lost to them.

This is a problem that will continue to fester without the direct involvement of Millennials. Simple solutions range from expanding taxes on Social Security to higher wage earners, to using a "means test" to determine whether wealthier Americans actually need Social Security to survive. Currently multi-millionaires receive Social Security just as the most needy do—except one group doesn't really need it to survive while the other does. And again, what about the needs of Millennials? As of 2018, Americans making more than $128,400 per year do not continue to pay social security taxes on all wage income.[44] This is inherently unfair to the vast number of Americans that will be relying on Social Security and it is extremely unfair to Millennials that are required to pay into the program without any assurances they too will benefit from it.

IMMIGRATION AND ICE

We Are Children of Immigrants

Give me your tired, your poor,
Your huddled masses yearning to breathe free.

– Emma Lazarus

The United States was established and built by immigrants. Europeans fleeing the Old World came to America seeking a better life, be it for religious freedom or economic opportunity (or both). Opportunities presented themselves during our Colonial Era for new immigrants to share in the benefits of building a "New American World." As President James Madison noted, "America was indebted to immigration for her settlement and prosperity. That part of America which had encouraged them most had advanced most rapidly in population, agriculture and the arts."

Yet, there has also been a powerful strain of isolationism and fear of newcomers to our shores, characterized by the way many immigrants have been mistreated—from African Americans who came here involuntarily as slaves to the Irish, Polish, Italian, Asian, Jewish and Hispanic populations—even when their arrival benefited the needs of American expansion in geography, agriculture and industry.

In 1882, Congress took measures to limit the influx of Asian immigrants via the Chinese Exclusion Acts for the first time. Such restrictions arose again in the 1920s to keep out people from less "desirable" areas (Asia, Africa, Central and South America). Little effort was undertaken to limit the influx of White Europeans, however, because of the belief they alone would appreciate America and assimilate easier into our economy and culture. This was nonsense, of course. Studies show that all immigrants assimilate into American culture within two generations.

Immigrants have appreciated that public educations and economic opportunities awaited those willing to learn and work hard. By the 1980s, the number of people seeking refuge and political asylum in America and those crossing our borders without authority increased dramatically. These undocumented immigrants, legally without "status," became labeled by the Far Right as "Illegals," allowing Conservatives to view them as criminals and "less deserving" than American citizens. Liberals and Progressives have a more charitable attitude. As a result, immigration has become a partisan issue in an effort to convince citizens that those choosing to come to America without visas somehow are a threat to the rest of us.

Since Donald Trump during his run for the presidency called undocumented immigrants from Hispanic countries "criminals and rapists" and claimed that they were a drain on public resources, there has been little rational discussion. After his election, inflammatory rhetoric escalated to policies of draconian measures in the name of "national security." All without merit. Studies indicate that undocumented immigrants are more law-abiding and less likely to commit crimes than American citizens. According to Giovanni Peri, an economist at the University of California, Davis, undocumented immigrants actually complement skilled American workers taking less desirable (yet much-needed) jobs. Immigrants are often the bedrock of our communities: They own the small business on the corner, they work in agriculture helping to feed the community, they pay their taxes, they commit crimes at lower rates than citizens, and they're just trying to build a better life for their children.[45] Americans supporting a crackdown on immigration from Hispanic countries might also be surprised to learn that most foreigners who come here and remain illegally after the expiration of their valid visas hail from European nations. But you won't hear that on Fox News because that doesn't fit the Right's narrative.

Even so, there are problems with our immigration system. The need for comprehensive immigration reform is not new. It has been a concern now for decades, yet conservative politicians continue to use it as a divisive talking point in their campaign rhetoric. When it comes to the issue of DREAMers, children who were brought into the United States by their parents and grew up here, Republican operatives cynically use them as political pawns. But DREAMers know no other country as their own, and think of themselves as Americans. They have shared classrooms, youth sports and church groups with native-born citizens all of their lives. They have fought with our troops in Afghanistan and Iraq and continue to serve in all areas of our military. They deserve permanent status and full citizenship in our country.

Some conservatives have bought into the dehumanizing rhetoric. Both President Reagan and, some years later, President George W. Bush, tried to address the issue by asking Congress to pass laws to deal with the issue, recognizing these children's contributions to American society. Yet, their efforts fell on deaf ears as Right-Wing cries of "amnesty" rang out. When President Obama delivered a speech mirroring Bush's address, seeking to spark Congressional action on immigration reform, the Right-Wing media attacked him as being "un-American," willing to "destroy" immigration policy in an effort to win "future Democratic votes." Some even recently have declared separating children from their parents is acceptable merely because they aren't American children. As if Americans have more rights than others. (The Supreme Court ruled over 130 years ago that the Equal Protection provisions of the 14th Amendment apply to all "persons" not just citizens (Yick Wo v. Hopkins, 1886).

According to The Brookings Institute, America will become a "Minority White nation" in 2045.[46] This development scares Conservatives because it threatens to marginalize traditional White society. Wishing to maintain the status quo, Conservatives want to postpone the rise of non-whites to power. Their biggest fear is that all of the DREAMers and immigrants from south of the border, when granted citizenship, will then vote a straight Democratic ticket come election time. That fear is not unfounded, considering the way GOP officials and politicians have alienated and mistreated immigrants and minorities. According to Pew Research, Millennials today most likely will be voting Democrat. The reasons? The party aligns closer to Millennials goals and values.[47] The same is likely to be true for DREAMers and immigrants—it is a self-fulfilling prophecy.

This is the backdrop for the unconscionable policies pursued by the Trump administration, to apprehend all immigrants—even those seeking legal asylum. Such actions include arrest and detention in facilities better suited to quarantining animals than human beings. There is also growing evidence that rogue border agents abuse those arrested, with numerous allegations of rape and murder coming to light.[48] When ordered by a Federal Court to immediately reunite families separated by ICE, the Administration simply has ignored the orders, seeking a confrontation at the Appellate Court level.[49] These policies are truly Un-American, and we should all be willing to stand up and say so.

The conservative response is that these agencies are simply doing their job and serving a function, which isn't untrue, but their scale and scope has morphed dramatically since their creation. Currently, Customs and Border Patrol (CBP), in conjunction with ICE are tasked with securing the border and preventing "illegal" immigration. Created in 2003 in response to the attacks on 9/11, ICE's role has expanded greatly under the Trump Administration, to the point where the agency now acts as an unbridled and sometimes rogue agency fully vested to arrest, deport and intern thousands of immigrants—some seeking to enter the country legally and some seeking legal asylum—without distinguishing between the two and often times without providing proper due process. This betrays America's long-standing principle of inviting immigrants and encouraging them to participate in the pursuit of the "American Dream."

In some cases, ICE has started to question the legitimate status of native-born Americans by rejecting documented proof of their birth in the United States. And it does not end here. Now the State Department under the Trump Administration has begun questioning the legal status and citizenship of Americans of Hispanic descent. On more than one occasion, ICE has detained and separated American citizens who happen to be of Mexican-American heritage. Where do we draw the line on such action? Will our government begin to question the rights of Citizens critical of the Administration?[50] The endeavor has become so large that the Trump Administration secretly shifted millions from FEMA Disaster aid funds to enlarge ICE's detention facilities. Additionally, the Administration, with the support of the GOP, has begun efforts to cut back on the number of refugees allowed by law for entry into America and has undertaken curbing legal immigration numbers.[51]

Many Boomers and Millennials have concluded that the unrestricted behavior of ICE violates Due Process of those caught in its web. Although immigration reform has been a long-standing issue, it's now past time for Congress to fully address and reform it. Continuing to use it as a divisive political issue has far too much of a human cost to allow it to continue unchecked. In the meantime, the policies and actions of ICE deserve Congressional and Judicial scrutiny leading to major reforms, or at least a call to abolish ICE, and start with something new that recognizes immigrants are not less human than Americans. When it comes to DREAMers, a pathway to permanent status only makes common sense as we all seek to attain the American Dream.

VOTING RIGHTS

Suppression Is Un-American

*So long as I do not firmly and irrevocably possess the right
to vote I do not possess myself. I cannot make up
my mind—it is made up for me. I cannot live as a
democratic citizen, observing the laws I have helped
to enact—I can only submit to the edict of others.*

—Dr. Martin Luther King Jr.

Voter suppression efforts are alive and well in America. For the past several decades, the GOP has been engaged in a concerted effort to disenfranchise black voters wherever possible.[52] This has not always been the case. After all, it was the Party of Lincoln that pushed for the passage of the Fifteenth Amendment to the Constitution, guaranteeing African Americans the right to vote.

It has also engaged in continued efforts to confuse the electorate regarding the real history of discrimination when it came to access to the voting booth. In Pre-Revolutionary America, all white male citizens could vote. In some colonies, women were extended that right as well. To consolidate its power, the white upper class soon unilaterally decided that only those owning property had the right to access the ballot box. While that should have included women—in early colonial Virginia, some of them owned land and acted as executor of their deceased husband's estate—ultimately the male leaders determined it best that women would not be able to acquire property, even if they inherited it.

Eventually, this fight would take to the national stage with the emergence of the Women's Suffrage movement and the ratification of the Nineteenth Amendment in 1920. Many of the leaders of this movement, however, routinely ignored the plight of African-American women who should have been granted the right to vote with the passage of the Fifteenth Amendment to the Constitution. In fact, efforts by Whites to keep African-Americans of both genders from voting were the hallmarks of the Jim Crow era in the South.

In the Northern states, discrimination was prevalent, too, but limiting the rights of Blacks to vote was not rooted in actual laws passed by state houses. Physically intimidating African-Americans to prevent them from voting did not require legislation. But in the South, actual laws were passed, requiring "intelligence" or "literacy" tests and the paying of poll taxes to cast one's vote.[53]

Following the passage of the Twenty-Fourth Amendment, which outlawed poll taxes, the 1965 Voting Rights Act was intended to end all voter discrimination against African-Americans. Subsequent efforts by the Department of Justice curtailed many attempts to circumvent the law and deny African-Americans access to the voting booth. For the past decade, however, the GOP has been engaged in steering state legislation against granting such access.

Voter Suppression comes in a variety of forms, but the GOP-led States lead the way in making voting more of a privilege than the fundamental Right it really is.

The most common form of suppression is the abusive practice of "gerrymandering" legislative districts in a way to marginalize the voting bloc minorities should benefit from. Although both political parties traditionally took advantage of gerrymandering, more contemporary strategies by GOP State Houses have led the efforts to carve out legislative districts in a way that splinters concentrations of minorities so they do not have the voting bloc they deserve. And these efforts have really paid off in the election of U.S. Representatives via manipulated Single Member Voting Districts.

Another approach has been to claim massive voter fraud—with no credible evidence whatsoever—instituting strict voter ID laws that are cumbersome for minorities to abide by. Whether that's as a result of not having the proper ID, or not having access to information instructing them on how to go acquire the proper ID with adequate time before the election, the end result is nearly the same: minority voters aren't able to vote.[54] Republicans also make it increasingly difficult for students to vote while away at college or university, minimizing the youth turnout in potential swing districts.[55]

Other recent attempts to lower turnout in some states include curtailing early voting, closing polling locations in predominantly minority areas, and eliminating early Sunday voting—a traditional method of getting African-American "Souls To The Polls" by promoting voting following church services.[56] In many GOP-led districts, access to the voting booth has been curtailed by providing countless voting locations in predominately white (and Conservative) districts while minority districts receive only a few, forcing African-American voters to wait in longer lines, increasing the likelihood that they will drop-out due to other obligations, or not show up at all.[57] On election day, it's not uncommon for polling places in minority districts to close when voting machines break down (without replacements available), while predominantly white districts have an ample supply of backup machines.[58]

Millennials, generally speaking, see through the charade of Republican led voter suppression efforts. Using information and technologies already available, there are specific reforms that could be instituted nationwide to dramatically increase voter turnout—notably, automatic voter registration, ranked choice Voting, voting from home and making Election Day a national holiday.

The simplest way to institute Automatic Voter Registration would be to send all U.S. citizens a Voter Registration card when they turn 18, at the same time they receive a Draft Registration Card (yes, these still exist).[59] If the government is capable of sending everyone a Draft Registration Card, why can't it send a Voter Registration Card? If everyone signs up automatically, the roadblocks to registering would be removed, and more people would be able to participate in the process.

Next, Ranked-Choice Voting is the concept that, in addition to selecting their preferred candidate, voters should be able to pick their top second and/or third choices as well. If their #1 choice doesn't win, their votes automatically go to their next top choice.

This would prevent any "spoiler-effect" from third-party candidates and reduce the apathy experienced by so many Millennials. The common refrain of "Well, my vote doesn't matter" would evaporate, because this simple reform would make everyone's vote count in accordance with their views and preferences. Maine recently enacted Ranked-Choice Voting, and the data clearly indicates an increase in voter satisfaction.[60]

Finally, our government needs to do a better job of allowing all eligible voters the opportunity to vote, even if they can't make it to the polls on election day or during an early voting period. Voting From Home works by mailing every registered voter a ballot and having them submit it by a specified deadline. It's simple, easy, and been proven to increase voter participation in the states that have made this a policy.[61]

Considering the problems with potential tampering with electronic voting machines, requiring a paper trail as backup to substantiate the voting totals would elevate confidence in our elections as well. There's no reason not to move in this direction.

Rhetoric is a poor substitute for action,
and we have trusted only to rhetoric.
If we are really to be a great nation,
we must not merely talk; we must act big.

— Theodore Roosevelt

★★ PART III ★★

Take Action!

Have a bias toward action—let's see something happen now. You can break that big plan into small steps and take the first step right away.
—Indira Gandhi

There is nothing wrong with America that cannot be cured with what is right in America.

—President Bill Clinton

As soon as Donald Trump began floating the campaign slogan "Make America Great Again," we began to wonder why this slogan had such a powerful effect on many people. What era, specifically, was he referencing when we were great?

Was it the 1980s when gay Americans were dying by the thousands during the AIDS epidemic? Was it the 1960s when we were sending our young men to die in Vietnam? Or the 1950s when more wildcat strikes occurred than ever before in our country, indicating unrest and discontent on the part of many Americans who were not living "Leave it to Beaver" lives? Or perhaps during the Jim Crow era in the South, from the late 1870s to the 1950s when blacks were disenfranchised and lynched? Or at the founding of our nation when most blacks were slaves and women had no enumerated rights and were relegated to a life of domesticity?

Trump's desire to return to a fantasy version of the past, instead of looking towards the future and building a vision for what we could be, was made possible by a general lack of knowledge of American history. While his demagoguery should have set off alarm bells immediately—and it did among many Democrats and progressives, and even a number of Republicans and libertarians—not enough people realized what a profound danger he represented to our country and cast their vote accordingly in the 2016 election. America has been great for more than two centuries now, not because it experienced golden ages in the past that we should want to return to, but because it evolved. With some setbacks and times of retrenchment, the over-all movement of our country has been to keep working to fulfill the promise and ideals enshrined in the Declaration of Independence: to realize the unalienable rights of life, liberty, the pursuit of happiness for all Americans.

Typically, politicians cite the fact that America has always had great aspirations and morals to strive towards. The guiding principles of the United States were always the claim to want to be better, to treat each other with dignity and respect, and to understand that no matter your race, gender, sexual orientation or circumstances at birth, if you work hard and play by the rules, you can get ahead in the United States. This is the essence of the American Dream, and this is far from what Donald Trump was preaching in his campaign.

His success signaled that we are, perhaps, merely going through a period of retrenchment again. A substantial number of Americans have been convinced by political operatives and their supporting media that our government in Washington is nothing more than a swamp of greedy operatives whose only purpose is to control the American electorate for their personal profit. Their arsenal of pro-paganda includes calling any effort to set the record straight "Fake News," telling outright lies, undermining our democratic institutions, and denigrating our system of government based on laws.

While there is certainly a lot to criticize about many of our elected officials, the cynicism against all government actually plays into the hands of the manipulators on the Right. Disaffected voters resulting in lower turnouts at election times helps them stay in power by rally-ing the people they have persuaded to their cause with false promises and a message based on fear, division, and anger.

How can Boomers and Millennials whose values are more in con-cert with those of our Founders and Framers combat this unfortunate development? Certainly not by wringing their hands, or becoming dispirited, depressed, and pessimistic.

We believe that the way forward is to affirm the democratic institutions that have served our country so well, in particular the Rule of Law. We believe that people should take political action. We believe that it behooves all of us to make our voices heard in as many ways as we can find. Ultimately, we are convinced that we must all cast our votes for candidates that will represent us, not just moneyed interest.

To accomplish that, we suggest a four-pronged approach:

- **Learn our great history**
- **Read the U.S. Constitution**
- **Get involved in progressive action**
- **Make your vote count**

There is no particular order in which to pursue these four areas, nor is it necessary to become an expert in any but one: Vote with a clear understanding of the implications—who you vote for and what that means. Vote for a candidate that fairly represents YOUR interests and the interests of America as a whole.

Learn our great history

Facts are stubborn things; and whatever may be our wishes, our inclinations, or the dictates of our passions, they cannot alter the state of facts and evidence.
—John Adams

Because America was built around personal freedom and a strong central government, it is vitally important for the entire electorate, and Millennials in particular, to learn more about our history and the foundations for our government created by our Founding Fathers and Framers. In this new age of "Alternative Facts," the time is ripe for our current and future leaders to know when politicians and their supporting media are manipulating history for their own purposes.

Knowing where we came from and how we got here is perhaps one of the most important pieces of knowledge we can carry with us as we look towards the imminent challenges facing future generations.

Right-Wing politicians and their media supporters don't just pursue an ideology driven agenda. They frequently spread outright lies—about our history, about the creating and meaning of the U.S. Constitution, about the development of American democracy, and about current events. They count on the electorate being ignorant and undereducated about the basic facts of American history.

Here are some whoppers in recent memory:

- *The United States was founded solely as a Christian Nation.* The Founders and Framers specifically recognized the importance of religious freedom—so much so that they protected the right to believe or not believe in organized religion in the First Amendment's Establishment Clause.

- *If we just cut taxes on job creators, their excess wealth will eventually trickle-down to the rest of us.* The concept of trickle-down economics, providing large tax cuts to corporations and wealthy, which will ultimately profit the working class—serving "Wall Street in order to benefit Main Street"—simply has never worked. Even the non-partisan Congressional Research Service, after reviewing over 60 years of tax policy, concluded that tax cuts for the wealthy never benefit the working poor. It's time to end this myth once and for all.[62]

- *School choice is the only way to educate our children.* This myth along with the bogus claim that "Liberals destroyed Public Education" has been circulated by Conservatives for quite a while and continues to rear its foolish head. Most educators, though, agree that the efforts to use standardized testing, while shifting public dollars to private testing companies, not only stunts actual learning by "teaching to the test" but also is cynically designed to use "Merit Pay" in an effort to attack teachers' unions. Horror stories abound about using inane standards to assess teacher performance that favors wealthier schools over impoverished ones, leading to the eventual closure of the latter.[63]

- *Liberals want to cut the military budget, leading to open borders and threatening your national security.* The United States spends $610 billion on military defense every year. This total is more than the budget of the next seven countries combined. Former Five Star General and President Dwight D. Eisenhower disagreed when he said, "In the councils of government, we must guard against the acquisition of unwarranted influence, whether sought or unsought, by the military-industrial complex. The potential for the disastrous rise of misplaced power exists and will persist." We should be investing our hard-earned tax dollars in our people, our crumbling infrastructure, and the future, not building bombs and tanks that the Pentagon isn't even asking for. [64]

- *Liberal spending programs will force our deficits to soar: We can't afford Social Security, Medicare, Medicaid, Meals on Wheels, etc.* It's more than a little ironic that with a bloated defense budget, and record deficits as a result of their tax schemes, Conservative always pull this tactic when it comes to Liberals' spending wishes. Never mind that they ignore the negative impacts of their bad spending habits. This has never been more evident than when Conservatives blocked economic stimulus programs proposed by Liberals in response to the 2008 Financial Crisis, only to "blow the budget" with huge deficit-fueling tax cuts as soon as Trump and the GOP got into power in 2016.[65]

In many cases, only knowledge and study about what happened decades and centuries ago can counter this barrage of "alternative facts" and "fake news."

But who can you believe? Certainly not talking heads or politicians with an agenda driven by holding on to power at all costs. Nor should you automatically trust people you like or because they happen to agree with your opinions. Go to the sources themselves. Read the original documents. Check out different interpreters of language and issues that may not be immediately accessible to you, and then make up your own mind. Look at the biographies of our Founding Fathers and Framers, both presidents and non-presidents alike (i.e. Washington, Franklin, Jefferson, Madison, Hamilton and others).

Check out George Washington's Farewell Address of 1796, for example (Appendix III). His discussion regarding the dangers of "factions" (by which he meant political parties) anticipates the divisive tribalism and gridlock we're witnessing in our government today.

By understanding how and why America's institutions were crafted by the Framers, the Millennial electorate will come to possess a knowledge currently not shared by many Boomers. In other words, don't take the media or a politician's view of history as accurate. Question every citation of alleged historical "fact" for accuracy and actively counter such statements with verifiable facts. Know your history and how your government was created and why.

You will find that many of the current hot issues—immigration, racism, slavery, voting rights, income inequality and more—have been discussed, debated and tossed around for many years. Some of what you'll discover will surprise you because we have been sold a bill of goods in the interests of benefiting certain factions. While we have touched on many facets of our history and government, this is not the place for us to present a primer of American history. That would require several books. But here is a list of essential topics:

- The Constitutional Convention—why it was needed after the first attempt at forming a government, based on the Articles of Confederation, failed

- The Constitution and its meaning with regards to Federalism vs State rights (the need for a strong central government vs. powerful individual state governments)

- How Chief Justice John Marshall in <u>Marbury vs Madison</u>, <u>Gibbons v. Ogden</u> and <u>McCulloch v. Maryland</u> shaped the Supreme Court's power and purpose

- The causes of the Civil War and the aftermath—Reconstruction and Jim Crow
- The Spanish American War, World War I and World War II, the Vietnam War
- A history of the Cold War to get an understanding of our relationship with Russia and the Soviet Union
- The history of social movements and protest in the United States.

It doesn't really matter where you begin. The point is to start educating yourself and make questioning the words and opinions of others a habit. Only a well-informed public can make good decisions at the ballot box.

Read the U.S. Constitution— The Articles and all 27 Amendments

We have the oldest written constitution still in force in the world, and it starts out with three words, We The People
—Ruth Bader Ginsburg

As a social contract laying the foundation for a government built on the rule of law, the U.S. Constitution is a remarkable document, both for its time and in and of itself. Until its creation in 1787 and ratification two years later, there had been only one other compact addressing human rights, the English Magna Carta. The "Great Charter" signed by King John at Runnymede in 1215 limited the authority of the monarch by safeguarding church rights and protecting the English barons against illegal and prolonged imprisonment, and assuring fair, swift trials. Curtailing the abuse of royal power, the document asserted a relationship between the king and his subjects based on feudal law. When it was finally accepted, it became a corner stone of the rights of individuals and the rights to justice.

Of course, the Magna Carta dealt with the individuals rights of the English aristocracy only. It took nearly six centuries before the Founders and Framers in America extended those rights universally to everyone via the U.S. Constitution, with some notable exceptions. The rights were accorded to men only—not women, Asian immigrants, or African-American slaves. The latter were also counted individually as only three-fifths of a man for census purposes to determine the number of representatives in Congress.

The original 1787 document said nothing about many of the rights for which the Constitution has become famous: freedom of speech, religion, assembly and the press; the right to bear arms; the right to a speedy and public trial; and the rights of individual states in relation to the federal government. They all were enumerated in the first ten amendments, the Bill of Rights, proposed and added during the fight over ratification.

In the process, an extraordinary document emerged. It not only provided the foundation for a government with checks and balances among its legislative, executive, and judicial branches, but it also included a mechanism for modification—the flexibility for adjustments required as times and values change.

Thus, amendments since passed ensured the end of slavery, granted African Americans and women the right to vote, and guaranteed the equal application of all Constitutional Rights to everyone—including non-citizens present on U.S. soil. A body of law built on these Articles and Amendments has extended human rights via Supreme Court decisions to end segregation in school, affirm a woman's right to have an abortion, legalize gay marriage in all States, and to fairly apply Due Process to everyone, not just citizens.

For more than 200 years, the experiment in democracy the Founders and Framers created has flourished, despite a Civil War, two World Wars, a major, nearly decade-long Depression, peaceful and violent protests, legal battles over various, important issues, and occasional attempts to subvert our democratic institutions. The U.S. Constitution has become a model for championing individual human rights in the context of a democratic government for many other countries, especially after World War II. Some of their constitutions extend more far-reaching individual rights to their citizens from the outset, but none have the experience or track record of allowing as large and diverse a country as the United States to thrive over time.

We live at a time when some Right-Wing organizations, politicians, and a president along with his supporters in the media are once again seeking to undermine and damage our democratic institutions to achieve their goals. That is why it is critical that everyone is well-informed about the rights and governmental system enshrined in the U.S. Constitution. It is the only way to fight back on a large scale and counter the frequent lies and assaults on our democratic principles by the current administration and its GOP enablers in Congress. Bringing court cases against abusive regulations, holding demonstrations nation-wide, and getting news from the Internet and liberal television stations are all very well. But we also need a more informed electorate.

Immigrants who want to become U. S. citizens have to pass a test consisting of 10 civic questions. Often, they know more about the Constitution than many native-born Americans. This needs to change. It would behoove Millennials, as the next generation yielding political power, to better understand the building blocks of our government and society. There is no better way to do that than to read the actual words of the Constitution.

For this reason, we have appended it and the Declaration of Independence to this book. It may take time, given the archaic quality of some of the language. If you get stuck, please feel compelled to look something up online or dig into some other books about the topic. With a more comprehensive understanding of the supreme law of our land, we can more easily counter the lies and deceptions practiced by the fear mongers and demagogues who care only about their own agendas.

Get involved in progressive action

The only thing necessary for the triumph of evil is for good men to do nothing.
– Edmund Burke

Many readers of this book may feel overwhelmed by everything that needs to be done. That is understandable, but shouldn't be a reason to sit back and do nothing. Getting upset about the state of affairs, yelling at the TV in frustration, rage-tweeting into the night might feel productive, but the real way to deal with times like these is to get politically involved. In something, anything.

There are good reasons beyond feeling like you're taking charge of your life. Gaining experience through action will allow you to learn how to get things done. It is ultimately more important to be for something than to rail or organize against.

The original Women's Suffragette Movement put all of its eggs in one basket. As a result, when the Nineteenth Amendment passed, guaranteeing women the right to vote, many of the supporters felt there was nothing left to be done. They partied during the Roaring Twenties, unaware that the system they joined would lead to the Great Depression. Or they went home, like Rosie the Riveter after World War II, who gave up the factory work and freedom she'd acquired and became a housewife again without asserting her independence (to be fair, there were some women who resented that returning male soldiers pushed them out their factory jobs). But taking part in a movement or going to work did not change them fundamentally. It took the second wave of the feminist movement in the 1970s to demonstrate for equal rights, equal pay, and abortion, and the #Me Too movement now to deal with sexual harassment.

The same thing happened to the Baby Boomers at the end of the Vietnam War. Many of the demonstrators who organized against the war and demonstrated in Washington became ordinary citizens—from corporate workers to self-employed professionals—pursuing their paychecks and careers during the "Me Decade" while becoming cogs in the system they had supposedly fought against.

The point is that the work doesn't finish because a particular issue gets resolved. Benjamin Franklin understood that. When asked what the delegates created during the Constitutional Convention, he said, "A Republic—if you can keep it!" That's why it's important to get involved and to develop the habit of working to make the world a better place for future generations. It doesn't require full-time engagement at every moment of one's life, although there are times when an all hands on deck approach is needed.

We are at one of those moments in history.

So, how do you get involved? It can be as simple as joining a community board, volunteering to help candidate get their platform known, participating in voting drives, accessing websites like *Millennial Politics*, making phone calls to Congressional leaders, etc.

Ultimately, it comes down to one thing above all others. While it should not be the only thing you do, right now, it is by far the most important:

Vote!

Make your vote count

Voting is how we participate in a civic society—be it for president, be it for a municipal election. It's the way we teach our children—in school elections—how to be citizens, and the importance of their voice.

– Loretta Lynch

A couple of elections ago, we heard a poll worker telling voters how much they appreciated voters taking advantage of their "privilege to vote." Please remember that a privilege is something someone grants to you because they could take it away. Voting is a RIGHT and it cannot be readily taken away. Be sure to exercise that right!

The fact that voting rights are under assault by the Right and its relentless efforts to disenfranchise African American voters should tell you how important voting is, not only in the 2018 midterms, but in all elections to come.

Put simply: It is how our democracy works. It's up to us. Our great republic is now in your hands.

AFTERWORD

The Boomer and the Millennial

Every generation inherits a world it never made; and,
as it does so, it automatically becomes the trustee of
that world for those who come after. In due course, each
generation makes its own accounting to its children.

—Robert Kennedy

As we sat down to write this book, we both had our own aims to address. The Boomer latched upon the notion that leadership is developed from the lessons learned and shared by an older generation to the younger one for their exploration and expansion. The Millennial on the other hand, took the position that America was fought for and developed by a small group of dedicated individuals yearning to create a better society. In the process, we realized that we share both visions that historical lessons must be learned but the new younger generation must be ready to take over leadership which is sorely needed in America today.

We recognize that not everyone will agree with our positions on every matter, and that is okay. We see our current political discourse as being toxic to our democracy as Americans have moved further and further apart from each other. Instead of talking to each other, we frequently find ourselves talking at each other. We hope the topics we have discussed in this book will bring forth further discussion and acceptance that we all want what is best for America. If that means adhering to less politically based ideology then so be it. America has faced many difficult challenges from across the ideological spectrum, and each time, we have overcome.

The challenges outlined in this book are by no means exhaustive. They cover only some of the most salient issues we will have to confront over the next 10 to 20 years. For example, we didn't touch on topics like advancing technologies, the threats posed by automation and artificial intelligence, and the future of potential job loss in vulnerable industries in our country and world-wide. These are big and thorny issues all of us will face and, instead of sticking our heads in the sand, we should take ownership of them and come to an agreement about how to best deal with them.

In order to do that successfully, however, we believe that any productive conversation or debate needs to be held in the context of these progressive values:

- *People should be valued over profit.*
- *Our climate and planet should be valued over corporate greed.*
- *Voters and constituents should be valued over special interests.*
- *Everyone should have access to lifesaving healthcare, without having to go broke to get it.*

When articulated as values instead of detailed policy statements, they ring true for most Americans. In the political arena, we need to recruit, train, and run candidates that hold these values shared by most. Together, we can make the changes needed for our country to be successful in the 21st Century.

Historically, it has been younger generations leading the way to move our country forward. For Millennials, it was their parents, the Boomers who protested against the war in Vietnam and pushed for Civil Rights, Voting rights, and an expansion of the social safety net. For Boomers, it was their parents who fought back the global rise of Fascism and Communism, and established the post-war order we all benefit from today. Now, it's the Millennials' turn to take the reins of our great republic.

As a country, we have pressing and urgent problems that must be dealt with. We're witnessing a power struggle between conservative Right-Wing and liberal-progressive views every day. From #MeToo, to Black Lives Matter, to calls for Constitutional Gun Reform and March For Our Lives, Millennials have started to respond to the most appalling instances and events which have been met with "business as usual" attitudes by those in power.

Now is the time for young people to get even more active. This means Millennials need to not only pay attention and vote; Millennials must get active, run for office, demonstrate against intolerance, and engage in peaceful civil disobedience when needed.

It also means not giving up when initial efforts to effect change fail. As Franklin D. Roosevelt once famously replied when asked how long it will take to bring America out of the Great Depression, "Take a method and try it. If it fails, admit it frankly, and try another. But by all means, try something."

The initial protests against the War in Vietnam were largely conducted by a minority of students and activists with little support from the general population. But by 1973, more than 70% of the general public, including a sizeable portion of Nixon's so called "Silent majority," were against the war. The big march on Washington that year included many older members who had been hawks after World War II and Korea. In time, they decided that the Vietnam War was not a just war or justifiable cause. As Millennials begin to lead, many independent and progressive Boomers will join.

Repeating the same mistakes without trying new approaches is not what America has stood for since it declared its independence in July of 1776. Change is inevitable. We must embrace it. Get involved. Pursue your interests and demand our leaders protect them. If politicians fail, elect new ones. We need action now. If you have a gripe and want to see something changed, don't just talk about it; do something about it. People often underestimate the influence they have and the power they can wield. Effecting positive change is in your control. Your voice is powerful, and your vote matters.

And concerned citizens turned activists are the most powerful group there is, and also the most-likely to make change.

From the Women's Suffrage Movement, to the fight for Civil Rights, to ending the Vietnam War, fighting to save lives during the HIV/AIDS crisis, to the fight for same-sex marriage, and the Occupy Wall Street Movement, the Movement For Black Lives, and then the Women's March; everyday ordinary people got involved, got active, and are no longer accepting the things they cannot change. They are changing the things they cannot accept.

And now it's on Millennials, and it's on you. Together we can do this. We believe democracy demands it.

ACKNOWLEDGMENTS

From the Boomer

I would like to acknowledge the contributions my son Nathan has made to the writing of this book. A father could never be prouder when realizing the positive impact he has made on his children. I have taught my children many lessons and it is a profound gift to know that not only have they learned those lessons well, but to realize they are now in a position to teach me new perspectives as well! It has been a pleasure working with Nathan on this book and for recognizing his perspective has validity and great value. I'm proud of everything he has done to become a concerned advocate for what is right and what is needed to improve the lives of all Americans.

To our editor, Chris Angermann who has believed in this book since the notion of working with both head-strong authors arose. Many thanks for pushing this project to its successful completion.

To my daughter, Aaryn, her husband Dr. Ephraim Hollander, and my grandchildren, Moshe, Dovy, Hannah and Simmy—may America always stay strong and be the leader in freedom for you and your children. To my daughter-in-law, Arielle, for helping to complete Nathan and for keeping it "real" for him.

To my wife Shellie Fay: the beat just keeps going. I am blessed to have you as my life-long partner.

To Susan and Erik Angermann who read the manuscript in its later stages and offered salient suggestions.

To all those dedicated to keeping America strong and moored to the ideals that our Founders and Framers intended for us.

And ultimately, to Hashem for making the words so easy to write.

Daniel R. Rubin

From the Millennial

While it may be cliche, I would be remiss if I didn't start by acknowledging the contributions of my co-author and father to this book as well as his influence on the trajectory of my life.

Being born into my family took no skill on my end, but it often makes me think of the famous Lou Gehrig quote at Yankee Stadium: "Today, I consider myself, one of the luckiest men on the face of this Earth." Thank you, Dad, for all of the sacrifices, support, and wisdom that you've provided me over the years.

To our editor, Chris, thank you for putting up with us. In times of challenge, you pushed back; often meeting fire with fire, and ultimately, I believe you helped make the sum total of this book better than its individual parts.

To my wife, Arielle, thank you for bearing with me through the early mornings, long nights, and boring weekends. Not only have you supported me in my (perhaps ill-conceived) efforts to write this book, but also in my (seemingly never-ending) pursuit of building *Millennial Politics*.

To my mom, Shellie, sister, Aaryn, brother-in-law, Ephraim, nephews and nieces, and my in-laws, Morty and Esther, and sister-in-law, Sarah, thank you for your unwavering support and unconditional love.

To my teammates at *Millenial Politics*: Jordan Valerie, Dylan Kristine, Pat Diemert, Jesse Barba, Heidi Cuda, and all others who have helped, thank you for all your efforts in shining a spotlight on progressive candidates, causes, and organizations.

In a roundabout way, this book would not have been possible without *Millennial Politics*. And *Millennial Politics* would not have been possible without you all. Thank you.

And last, to those who have been working in politics for decades, and to those who are just getting involved now: I'm glad to have you by my side. Together, we can (and will) do great things. Let's go usher in a new Progressive Era. Onward.

Nathan H. Rubin

ENDNOTES

1. Confessore, Nicholas. "Koch Brothers' Budget of $889 Million for 2016 Is on Par With Both Parties' Spending." *The New York Times*, The New York Times, 26 Jan. 2015, www.nytimes.com/2015/01/27/us/politics/kochs-plan-to-spend-900-million-on-2016-campaign.html.

2. Nilsen, Ella. "A New Report Says Democrats Need to Win the Popular Vote by 11 Points to Retake the House." *Vox*, Vox, 27 Mar. 2018, www.vox.com/policy-and-politics/2018/3/27/17144198/gerrymandering-brennan-center-report-midterms-democrats-house-2018.

3. Goldschein, Eric. "10 Fake Grassroots Movements Started By Corporations To Sway Your Opinion." *Business Insider*, Business Insider, 30 Sept. 2011, www.businessinsider.com/astroturfing-grassroots-movements-2011-9#exxon-mobil-was-behind-a-youtube-video-spoofing-al-gores-an-inconvenient-truth-1.

4. Friedman, Zack. "Student Loan Debt Statistics In 2018: A $1.5 Trillion Crisis." *Forbes*, Forbes Magazine, 13 June 2018, www.forbes.com/sites/zackfriedman/2018/06/13/student-loan-debt-statistics-2018/.

5. CSPAN. "Sen. James Inhofe (R-OK) Snowball in the Senate (C-SPAN)." CSPAN, 26 Feb. 2015, www.youtube.com/watch?v=3E0a_60PMR8.

6. Runciman, David. "How Climate Scepticism Turned into Something More Dangerous." *The Guardian*, Guardian News and Media, 7 July 2017, www.theguardian.com/environment/2017/jul/07/climate-change-denial-scepticism-cynicism-politics.

7. Goodell, Jeff. *The Water Will Come: Rising Seas, Sinking Cities, and the Remaking of the Civilized World*. Little, Brown and Company, 2017.

8. Hao, Karen. "Renewable Energy Is Creating US Jobs Twice as Fast as Any Other Industry." *Quartz*, Quartz, 26 Oct. 2017, http://qz.com/1111998/renewable-energy-is-creating-us-jobs-twice-as-fast-as-any-other-industry/.

9   "Analysis | Flooding in Miami Is No Longer News - but It's Certainly Newsworthy." *The Washington Post*, WP Company, 4 Aug. 2017, www.washingtonpost.com/news/politics/wp/2017/08/04/flooding-in-miami-is-no-longer-news-but-its-certainly-newsworthy/.

10 "Felony Disenfranchisement Laws (Map)." *American Civil Liberties Union*, American Civil Liberties Union, www.aclu.org/issues/voting-rights/voter-restoration/felony-disenfranchisement-laws-map.

11 Smith, Jamil. "Jamil Smith: Lessons From a Botched Voter Suppression Scheme." *Rolling Stone*, Rolling Stone, 28 Aug. 2018, www.rollingstone.com/politics/politics-news/georgia-voter-suppression-scheme-716393/.

12 ACLU Staff. "Racial Disparities in Sentencing." *ACLU.com*, American Civil Liberties Union, 27 Oct. 2014, https://www.aclu.org/sites/default/files/assets/141027_iachr_racial_disparities_aclu_submission_0.pdf.

13 Alexander, Michelle. "More Black Men Are In Prison Today Than Were Slaves In 1850, Law Professor Says." *The Huffington Post*, HuffingtonPost.com, 13 Oct. 2011, www.huffingtonpost.com/2011/10/12/michelle-alexander-more-black-men-in-prison-slaves-1850_n_1007368.html.

14 "Philadelphia DA Larry Krasner Promised a Criminal Justice Revolution. He's Exceeding Expectations." *The Intercept*, The Intercept, 20 Mar. 2018, http://theintercept.com/2018/03/20/larry-krasner-philadelphia-da/.

15 Levin, Sam, and Olivia Solon. "Zuckerberg Defends Facebook Users' Right to Be Wrong—Even Holocaust Deniers." *The Guardian*, Guardian News and Media, 18 July 2018, www.theguardian.com/technology/2018/jul/18/zuckerberg-facebook-holocaust-deniers-censorship.

16 Decker, Cathleen, and Michael A. Memoli. "Man Inspired by False 'Pizzagate' Rumor on Internet Pleads Guilty to Shooting at D.C. Restaurant." Los Angeles Times, Los Angeles Times, 24 Mar. 2017, www.latimes.com/nation/nationnow/la-na-pizzagate-shooting-20170324-story.html.

17 "Analysis | President Trump Has Made 3,251 False or Misleading Claims in 497 Days." *The Washington Post*, WP Company, 1 June 2018, www.washingtonpost.com/news/fact-checker/wp/2018/06/01/president-trump-has-made-3251-false-or-misleading-claims-in-497-days/.

18 "The Extraordinary Number of Kids Who Have Endured School Shootings since Columbine." T*he Washington Post*, WP Company, www.washingtonpost.com/graphics/2018/local/us-school-shootings-history/?utm_term=.fed244a1e9fc.

19 Wallace, Lacey. "Why Is There so Little Research on Guns in the US? 6 Questions Answered." *The Conversation*, The Conversation, 14 Sept. 2018, http://theconversation.com/why-is-there-so-little-research-on-guns-in-the-us-6-questions-answered-92163.

20 "DeVos Says Safety Committee Formed after School Shootings Won't Study Guns." *NBCNews.com*, NBCUniversal News Group, www.nbcnews.com/news/us-news/betsy-devos-says-safety-committee-formed-after-school-shootings-won-n880271.

21 USC Section 5845(b), 27 CFR Sections 478.11 & 479.11.

22 Haag, Matthew. "The Equal Rights Amendment Was Just Ratified by Illinois. What Does That Mean?" The New York Times, The New York Times, 31 May 2018, www.nytimes.com/2018/05/31/us/equal-rights-amendment-illinois.html.

23 Chatterjee, Rhitu. "A New Survey Finds 81 Percent Of Women Have Experienced Sexual Harassment." *NPR*, NPR, 22 Feb. 2018, www.npr.org/sections/thetwo-way/2018/02/21/587671849/a-new-survey-finds-eighty-percent-of-women-have-experienced-sexual-harassment.

24 Beusman, Callie. "A State-by-State List of the Lies Abortion Doctors Are Forced to Tell Women." *Broadly*, VICE, 18 Aug. 2016, https://broadly.vice.com/en_us/article/nz88gx/a-state-by-state-list-of-the-lies-abortion-doctors-are-forced-to-tell-women.

25 Parenthood, Planned. "How Federal Funding Works at Planned Parenthood." *Planned Parenthood Action Fund*, https://www.istandwithpp.org/defund-defined/how-federal-funding-works-planned-parenthood.

26 Lopez, German. "How Most States Allow Discrimination against LGBTQ People." *Vox*, Vox, 19 Aug. 2016, www.vox.com/2015/4/22/8465027/lgbt-nondiscrimination-laws.

27 Hiltzik, Michael. "The Supreme Court's Awful Hobby Lobby Decision Just Spawned a Very Ugly Stepchild." *Los Angeles Times*, Los Angeles Times, 19 Aug. 2016, http://www.latimes.com/business/hiltzik/la-fi-hiltzik-hobby-child-20160819-snap-story.html.

28 United States Government. "A Timeline of HIV and AIDS." HIV.gov, 10 Sept. 2018, www.hiv.gov/hiv-basics/overview/history/hiv-and-aids-timeline.H

29 Shwarz, Hunter. "Obama and Clinton Love to Celebrate Gay Marriage Now. Here's How Late They Were to the Party." The Washington Post, WP Company, 26 June 2015, www.washingtonpost.com/news/the-fix/wp/2015/06/26/obama-and-clinton-love-to-celebrate-gay-marriage-now-heres-how-late-they-were-to-the-party/.

30 Badger, Emily. "How Redlining's Racist Effects Lasted for Decades." *The New York Times*, The New York Times, 24 Aug. 2017, www.nytimes.com/2017/08/24/upshot/how-redlinings-racist-effects-lasted-for-decades.html.

31 Sanchez, Claudio. "The Charter School Vs. Public School Debate Continues." *NPR*, NPR, 16 July 2013, www.npr.org/2013/07/16/201109021/the-charter-school-vs-public-school-debate-continues.

32 Friedman, Zack. "Student Loan Debt Statistics In 2018: A $1.5 Trillion Crisis." *Forbes*, Forbes Magazine, 13 June 2018, www.forbes.com/sites/zackfriedman/2018/06/13/student-loan-debt-statistics-2018/#6ad-0ca2c7310.

33 Odland, Steve. "College Costs Out Of Control." *Forbes*, Forbes Magazine, 15 May 2012, www.forbes.com/sites/steveodland/2012/03/24/college-costs-are-soaring/#12b1a0cb1f86.

34 Fortin, Jacey, and Jonah Engel Bromwich. "Sinclair Made Dozens of Local News Anchors Recite the Same Script." *The New York Times*, The New York Times, 2 Apr. 2018, www.nytimes.com/2018/04/02/business/media/sinclair-news-anchors-script.html.

35 Burgess, Matt. "What Is GDPR? The Summary Guide to GDPR Compliance in the UK." *WIRED*, WIRED UK, 11 July 2018, www.wired.co.uk/article/what-is-gdpr-uk-eu-legislation-compliance-summary-fines-2018.

36 Locker, Melissa. "The Problem with Trump's Tweet about South Africa." *Fast Company*, Fast Company, 23 Aug. 2018, www.fastcompany.com/90224283/trumps-south-africa-tweet-the-problem-with-his-large-scale-killing-of-farmers-claim.

37 Gallup, Inc. "Data Security: Not a Big Concern for Millennials." Gallup.com, 9 June 2016, www.gallup.com/businessjournal/192401/data-security-not-big-concern-millennials.aspx.

38 United States Government. "COINTELPRO." FBI, Federal Bureau of Investigations, 5 May 2011, http://vault.fbi.gov/cointel-pro.

39 Mataconis, Doug. "Mark Zuckerberg Tries To Explain The Internet To Elderly Senators." Outside the Beltway, 11 Apr. 2018, www.outsidethe-beltway.com/mark-zuckerberg-tries-to-explain-the-internet-to-elder-ly-senators/.

40 Kingseed, Wyatt. "The 'Bonus Army' War in Washington." HistoryNet, History Net, 24 Jan. 2018, www.historynet.com/the-bonus-army-war-in-washington.htm.

41 United States Government. "Social Security." Reports, Facts and Figures | Press Office | Social Security Administration, Social Security Administration, www.ssa.gov/history/briefhistory3.html.

42 Meister, Jeanne. "The Future Of Work: Job Hopping Is the 'New Normal' for Millennials." *Forbes*, Forbes Magazine, 3 Jan. 2017, www.forbes.com/sites/jeannemeister/2012/08/14/the-future-of-work-job-hopping-is-the-new-normal-for-millennials/#3b19879b13b8.

43 Goss, Stephen C. "Social Security Administration." Reports, Facts and Figures | Press Office | Social Security Administration, 1 Aug. 2010, www.ssa.gov/policy/docs/ssb/v70n3/v70n3p111.html.

44 Bieber, Christy. "What Is the 2018 Maximum Social Security Tax?" The Motley Fool, The Motley Fool, 10 Dec. 2017, www.fool.com/invest-ing/2017/12/10/what-is-the-2018-maximum-social-security-tax.aspx.

45 Davidson, Adam. "Do Illegal Immigrants Actually Hurt the U.S. Economy?" *The New York Times*, The New York Times, 12 Feb. 2013, https://www.nytimes.com/2013/02/17/magazine/do-illegal-immigrants-actu-ally-hurt-the-us-economy.html.

46 Frey, William H. "The US Will Become 'Minority White' in 2045, Census Projects." *Brookings*, Brookings, 10 Sept. 2018, https://www.brookings.edu/blog/the-avenue/2018/03/14/the-us-will-become-minority-white-in-2045-census-projects/.

47 Jones, Bradley. "Trends in Party Affiliation among Demographic Groups | Pew Research Center." *Pew Research Center for the People and the Press*, Pew Research Center for the People and the Press, 18 Sept. 2018, http://www.people-press.org/2018/03/20/1-trends-in-party-af-filiation-among-demographic-groups/.

48 Romero, Simon, and Manny Fernandez. "Border Patrol Agent Arrested in Connection With Murders of 4 Women." *The New York Times*, The New York Times, 15 Sept. 2018, https://www.nytimes.com/2018/09/15/us/laredo-border-patrol-agent-arrested.html.

49 Silva, Daniella. "Judge Orders U.S. to Reunite Families Separated at the Border. What Now?" *NBCNews.com*, NBCUniversal News Group, https://www.nbcnews.com/news/us-news/u-s-ordered-reunite-migrant-families-now-what-n887096.

50 Sieff, Kevin. "U.S. Is Denying Passports to Americans along the Border, Throwing Their Citizenship into Question." *The Washington Post*, WP Company, 13 Sept. 2018, https://www.washingtonpost.com/world/the_americas/us-is-denying-passports-to-americans-along-the-border-throwing-their-citizenship-into-question/2018/08/29/1d630e84-a0da-11e8-a3dd-2a1991f075d5_story.html?utm_term=.8c52f3b88e26.

51 Hauslohner, Abigail, and Andrew Ba Tran. "Trump Is Making Inroads in Reducing Legal Immigration." *Chicagotribune.com*, Chicago Tribune Company, 3 July 2018, http://www.chicagotribune.com/news/nation-world/ct-legal-migration-steep-decrease-20180702-story.html and https://www.nytimes.com/2018/09/17/us/politics/trump-refugees-historic-cuts.html.

52 Graham, David A. "North Carolina's Deliberate Discrimination Against Black Voters." *The Atlantic*, Atlantic Media Company, 30 July 2016, www.theatlantic.com/politics/archive/2016/07/north-carolina-voting-rights-law/493649/.

53 Public Broadcasting Service. "The Rise and Fall of Jim Crow. Tools and Activities | PBS." Thirteen: Media With Impact, Public Broadcasting Service (PBS), www.thirteen.org/wnet/jimcrow/voting_literacy.html.

54 Berman, Ari. "How the GOP Rigs Elections." *Rolling Stone*, Rolling Stone, 25 June 2018, www.rollingstone.com/politics/politics-news/how-the-gop-rigs-elections-121907/.

55 Wheeler, Lydia. "GOP Bill Scraps Voter Registration Requirements for Colleges." *The Hill*, The Hill, 14 Dec. 2017, http://thehill.com/regulation/other/364793-gop-bill-scraps-voter-registration-requirements-for-colleges.

56 Lopez, German. "7 Specific Ways States Made It Harder for Americans to Vote in 2016." *Vox*, Vox, 7 Nov. 2016, www.vox.com/policy-and-politics/2016/11/7/13545718/voter-suppression-early-voting-2016.

57 Wolf, Richard, and Kevin McCoy. "Voters in Key States Endured Long Lines, Equipment Failures." *USA Today*, Gannett Satellite Information Network, 9 Nov. 2016, www.usatoday.com/story/news/politics/elections/2016/11/08/voting-polls-election-day/93201770/.

58 CBS News. "Voting Issues Reported at Polling Places on Election Day." *CBS News*, CBS Interactive, 8 Nov. 2016, www.cbsnews.com/news/live-updates-voting-issues-reported-at-polling-places-on-election-day/.

59 United States Government. "Selective Service Draft Registration." Selective Service System, U.S. Government, www.sss.gov/Registration/Why-Register.

60 Gordon, Clay. "Maine's Sec. of State on Lessons-Learned, Cost of Ranked-Choice Voting." *WCSH*, News Center Maine, 23 June 2018, www.newscentermaine.com/article/news/local/maines-sec-of-state-on-lessons-learned-cost-of-ranked-choice-voting/97-566900852.

61 Edelman, Gilad, and Paul Glastris. "Analysis | Letting People Vote at Home Increases Voter Turnout. Here's Proof." *The Washington Post*, WP Company, 26 Jan. 2018, www.washingtonpost.com/outlook/letting-people-vote-at-home-increases-voter-turnout-heres-proof/2018/01/26/d637b9d2-017a-11e8-bb03-722769454f82_story.html.

62 Ungar, Rick. "Non-Partisan Congressional Tax Report Debunks Core Conservative Economic Theory-GOP Suppresses Study." *Forbes*, Forbes Magazine, 4 Nov. 2012, https://www.forbes.com/sites/rickungar/2012/11/02/non-partisan-congressional-tax-report-debunks-core-conservative-economic-theory-gop-suppresses-study/#5c044f9a22e6.

63 Strauss, Valerie. "Analysis | 34 Problems with Standardized Tests." *The Washington Post*, WP Company, 19 Apr. 2017, https://www.washingtonpost.com/news/answer-sheet/wp/2017/04/19/34-problems-with-standardized-tests/?utm_term=.b96971e30710.

64 NPR Staff. "Ike's Warning Of Military Expansion, 50 Years Later." *NPR*, NPR, 17 Jan. 2011, https://www.npr.org/2011/01/17/132942244/ikes-warning-of-military-expansion-50-years-later.

65 Rappeport, Alan. "Republicans Learn to Love Deficit Spending They Once Loathed." *The New York Times*, The New York Times, 9 Feb. 2018, https://www.nytimes.com/2018/02/08/us/politics/republicans-spend-ing-deficits-debt.html0.

FURTHER READING

The Articles of Confederation

The Federalist Papers

George Washington, "Farewell Address"

Abraham Lincoln, "Gettysburg Address"

Frederick Douglass, "What to the Slave Is the Fourth of July?"

Progressive Party Platform of 1912

Brown v. Board of Education of Topeka I and II

John F. Kennedy, "Inaugural Address" (Jan. 1961)

Martin Luther King's *Letters from a Birmingham Jail*

Martin Luther King Jr., "I Have a Dream" speech

Lyndon B. Johnson, "Great Society" Speech.

History of Social Movements in America:

Daniel R. Rubin, *How Our Government Really Works, Despite What They Say*, Bardolf & Company, Sarasota, Florida

APPENDIX I

THE DECLARATION OF INDEPENDENCE

IN CONGRESS, July 4, 1776.

The unanimous Declaration of the thirteen United States of America:

When in the Course of human events, it becomes necessary for one people to dissolve the political bands which have connected them with another, and to assume among the powers of the earth, the separate and equal station to which the Laws of Nature and of Nature's God entitle them, a decent respect to the opinions of mankind requires that they should declare the causes which impel them to the separation.

We hold these truths to be self-evident, that all men are created equal, that they are endowed by their Creator with certain unalienable Rights, that among these are Life, Liberty and the pursuit of Happiness.—That to secure these rights, Governments are instituted among Men, deriving their just powers from the consent of the governed, — That whenever any Form of Government becomes destructive of these ends, it is the Right of the People to alter or to abolish it, and to institute new Government, laying its foundation on such principles and organizing its powers in such form, as to them shall seem most likely to effect their Safety and Happiness. Prudence, indeed, will dictate that Governments long established should not be changed for light and transient causes; and accordingly all experience hath shewn, that mankind are more disposed to suffer, while evils are sufferable, than to right themselves by abolishing the forms to which they are accustomed. But when a long train of abuses and usurpations, pursuing invariably the same Object evinces a design to reduce them under absolute Despotism, it is their right, it is their duty, to throw off such Government, and to provide new Guards for their future security.--Such has been the patient sufferance of these Colonies; and such is now the necessity which constrains them to alter their former Systems of Government. The history of the present King of Great Britain is a history of repeated injuries and usurpations, all having in direct object the establishment of an absolute Tyranny over these States. To prove this, let Facts be submitted to a candid world.

He has refused his Assent to Laws, the most wholesome and necessary for the public good.

He has forbidden his Governors to pass Laws of immediate and pressing importance, unless suspended in their operation till his Assent should be obtained; and when so suspended, he has utterly neglected to attend to them.

He has refused to pass other Laws for the accommodation of large districts of people, unless those people would relinquish the right of Representation in the Legislature, a right inestimable to them and formidable to tyrants only.

He has called together legislative bodies at places unusual, uncomfortable, and distant from the depository of their public Records, for the sole purpose of fatiguing them into compliance with his measures.

He has dissolved Representative Houses repeatedly, for opposing with manly firmness his invasions on the rights of the people.

He has refused for a long time, after such dissolutions, to cause others to be elected; whereby the Legislative powers, incapable of Annihilation, have returned to the People at large for their exercise; the State remaining in the mean time exposed to all the dangers of invasion from without, and convulsions within.

He has endeavoured to prevent the population of these States; for that purpose obstructing the Laws for Naturalization of Foreigners; refusing to pass others to encourage their migrations hither, and raising the conditions of new Appropriations of Lands.

He has obstructed the Administration of Justice, by refusing his Assent to Laws for establishing Judiciary powers.

He has made Judges dependent on his Will alone, for the tenure of their offices, and the amount and payment of their salaries.

He has erected a multitude of New Offices, and sent hither swarms of Officers to harrass our people, and eat out their substance.

He has kept among us, in times of peace, Standing Armies without the Consent of our legislatures.

He has affected to render the Military independent of and superior to the Civil power.

He has combined with others to subject us to a jurisdiction foreign to our constitution, and unacknowledged by our laws; giving his Assent to their Acts of pretended Legislation:

For Quartering large bodies of armed troops among us:

For protecting them, by a mock Trial, from punishment for any Murders which they should commit on the Inhabitants of these States:

For cutting off our Trade with all parts of the world:

For imposing Taxes on us without our Consent:

For depriving us in many cases, of the benefits of Trial by Jury:

For transporting us beyond Seas to be tried for pretended offences.

For abolishing the free System of English Laws in a neighbouring Province, establishing therein an Arbitrary government, and enlarging its Boundaries so as to render it at once an example and fit instrument for introducing the same absolute rule into these Colonies:

For taking away our Charters, abolishing our most valuable Laws, and altering fundamentally the Forms of our Governments:

For suspending our own Legislatures, and declaring themselves invested with power to legislate for us in all cases whatsoever.

He has abdicated Government here, by declaring us out of his Protection and waging War against us.

He has plundered our seas, ravaged our Coasts, burnt our towns, and destroyed the lives of our people.

He is at this time transporting large Armies of foreign Mercenaries to compleat the works of death, desolation and tyranny, already begun with circumstances of Cruelty & perfidy scarcely paralleled in the most barbarous ages, and totally unworthy the Head of a civilized nation.

He has constrained our fellow Citizens taken Captive on the high Seas to bear Arms against their Country, to become the executioners of their friends and Brethren, or to fall themselves by their Hands.

He has excited domestic insurrections amongst us, and has endeavoured to bring on the inhabitants of our frontiers, the merciless Indian Savages, whose known rule of warfare, is an undistinguished destruction of all ages, sexes and conditions.

In every stage of these Oppressions We have Petitioned for Redress in the most humble terms: Our repeated Petitions have been answered only by repeated injury. A Prince whose character is thus marked by every act which may define a Tyrant, is unfit to be the ruler of a free people.

Nor have We been wanting in attentions to our Brittish brethren. We have warned them from time to time of attempts by their legislature to extend an unwarrantable jurisdiction over us. We have reminded them of the circumstances of our emigration and settlement here. We have appealed to their native justice and magnanimity, and we have conjured them by the ties of our common kindred to disavow these usurpations, which, would inevitably interrupt our connections and correspondence. They too have been deaf to the voice of justice and of consanguinity. We must, therefore, acquiesce in the necessity, which denounces our Separation, and hold them, as we hold the rest of mankind, Enemies in War, in Peace Friends.

We, therefore, the Representatives of the united States of America, in General Congress, Assembled, appealing to the Supreme Judge of the world for the rectitude of our intentions, do, in the Name, and by Authority of the good People of these Colonies, solemnly publish and declare, That these United Colonies are, and of Right ought to be Free and Independent States; that they are Absolved from all Allegiance to the British Crown, and that all political connection between them and the State of Great Britain, is and ought to be totally dissolved; and that as Free and Independent States, they have full Power to levy War, conclude Peace, contract Alliances, establish Commerce, and to do all other Acts and Things which Independent States may of right do. And for the support of this Declaration, with a firm reliance on the protection of divine Providence, we mutually pledge to each other our Lives, our Fortunes and our sacred Honor.

The 56 signatures on the Declaration appear in the positions indicated:

Column 1:
    Georgia: Button Gwinnett, Lyman Hall, George Walton

Column 2:
    North Carolina: William Hooper, Joseph Hewes, John Penn
    South Carolina: Edward Rutledge, Thomas Heyward, Jr.,
        Thomas Lynch, Jr., Arthur Middleton

Column 3:
    Massachusetts: John Hancock
    Maryland: Samuel Chase, William Paca, Thomas Stone,
        Charles Carroll of Carrollton
    Virginia: George Wythe, Richard Henry Lee,
        Thomas Jefferson, Benjamin Harrison,
        Thomas Nelson, Jr., Francis Lightfoot Lee,
        Carter Braxton

Column 4
    Pennsylvania: Robert Morris, Benjamin Rush,
        Benjamin Franklin, John Morton, George Clymer
        James Smith, George Taylor, James Wilson
        George Ross
    Delaware: Caesar Rodney, George Read, Thomas McKean

Column 5
    New York: William Floyd, Philip Livingston, Francis Lewis
        Lewis Morris
    New Jersey: Richard Stockton, John Witherspoon
        Francis Hopkinson, John Hart, Abraham Clark

Column 6

New Hampshire: Josiah Bartlett, William Whipple
Massachusetts: Samuel Adams, John Adams
　　　　Robert Treat Paine, Elbridge Gerry
Rhode Island: Stephen Hopkins, William Ellery
Connecticut: Roger Sherman, Samuel Huntington
　　　　William Williams, Oliver Wolcott
New Hampshire: Matthew Thornton

APPENDIX II

THE CONSTITUTION OF THE UNITED STATES

We the People of the United States, in Order to form a more perfect Union, establish Justice, insure domestic Tranquility, provide for the common defence, promote the general Welfare, and secure the Blessings of Liberty to ourselves and our Posterity, do ordain and establish this Constitution for the United States of America.

Article I

Section 1

All legislative Powers herein granted shall be vested in a Congress of the United States, which shall consist of a Senate and House of Representatives.

Section 2

The House of Representatives shall be composed of Members chosen every second Year by the People of the several States, and the Electors in each State shall have the Qualifications requisite for Electors of the most numerous Branch of the State Legislature.

No Person shall be a Representative who shall not have attained to the Age of twenty five Years, and been seven Years a Citizen of the United States, and who shall not, when elected, be an Inhabitant of that State in which he shall be chosen.

Representatives and direct Taxes shall be apportioned among the several States which may be included within this Union, according to their respective Numbers, which shall be determined by adding to the whole Number of free Persons, including those bound to Service for a Term of Years, and excluding Indians not taxed, three fifths of all other Persons. The actual Enumeration shall be made within three Years after the first Meeting of the Congress of the United States, and within every subsequent Term of ten Years, in such Manner as they shall by Law direct. The Number of Representatives shall not exceed one for every thirty Thousand, but each State shall have at Least one Representative; and until such enumeration shall be made, the State of New Hampshire shall be entitled to chuse three, Massachusetts eight, Rhode-Island and Providence Plantations one, Connecticut five, New-York six, New Jersey four, Pennsylvania eight, Delaware one, Maryland six, Virginia ten, North Carolina five, South Carolina five, and Georgia three.

When vacancies happen in the Representation from any State, the Executive Authority thereof shall issue Writs of Election to fill such Vacancies.

The House of Representatives shall chuse their Speaker and other Officers; and shall have the sole Power of Impeachment.

Section 3

The Senate of the United States shall be composed of two Senators from each State, chosen by the Legislature thereof, for six Years; and each Senator shall have one Vote.

Immediately after they shall be assembled in Consequence of the first Election, they shall be divided as equally as may be into three Classes. The Seats of the Senators of the first Class shall be vacated at the Expiration of the second Year, of the second Class at the Expiration of the fourth Year, and of the third Class at the Expiration of the sixth Year, so that one third may be chosen every second Year; and if Vacancies happen by Resignation, or otherwise, during the Recess of the Legislature of any State, the Executive thereof may make temporary Appointments until the next Meeting of the Legislature, which shall then fill such Vacancies.4

No Person shall be a Senator who shall not have attained to the Age of thirty Years, and been nine Years a Citizen of the United States, and who shall not, when elected, be an Inhabitant of that State for which he shall be chosen.

The Vice President of the United States shall be President of the Senate, but shall have no Vote, unless they be equally divided.

The Senate shall chuse their other Officers, and also a President pro tempore, in the Absence of the Vice President, or when he shall exercise the Office of President of the United States.

The Senate shall have the sole Power to try all Impeachments. When sitting for that Purpose, they shall be on Oath or Affirmation. When the President of the United States is tried, the Chief Justice shall preside: And no Person shall be convicted without the Concurrence of two thirds of the Members present.

Judgment in Cases of impeachment shall not extend further than to removal from Office, and disqualification to hold and enjoy any Office of honor, Trust or Profit under the United States: but the Party convicted shall nevertheless be liable and subject to Indictment, Trial, Judgment and Punishment, according to Law.

Section 4

The Times, Places and Manner of holding Elections for Senators and Representatives, shall be prescribed in each State by the Legislature thereof; but the Congress may at any time by Law make or alter such Regulations, except as to the Places of chusing Senators.

The Congress shall assemble at least once in every Year, and such Meeting shall be on the first Monday in December, unless they shall by Law appoint a different Day.

Section 5

Each House shall be the Judge of the Elections, Returns and Qualifications of its own Members, and a Majority of each shall constitute a Quorum to do Business; but a smaller Number may adjourn from day to day, and may be authorized to compel the Attendance of absent

Members, in such Manner, and under such Penalties as each House may provide.

Each House may determine the Rules of its Proceedings, punish its Members for disorderly Behaviour, and, with the Concurrence of two thirds, expel a Member.

Each House shall keep a Journal of its Proceedings, and from time to time publish the same, excepting such Parts as may in their Judgment require Secrecy; and the Yeas and Nays of the Members of either House on any question shall, at the Desire of one fifth of those Present, be entered on the Journal.

Neither House, during the Session of Congress, shall, without the Consent of the other, adjourn for more than three days, nor to any other Place than that in which the two Houses shall be sitting.

Section 6

The Senators and Representatives shall receive a Compensation for their Services, to be ascertained by Law, and paid out of the Treasury of the United States. They shall in all Cases, except Treason, Felony and Breach of the Peace, be privileged from Arrest during their Attendance at the Session of their respective Houses, and in going to and returning from the same; and for any Speech or Debate in either House, they shall not be questioned in any other Place.

No Senator or Representative shall, during the Time for which he was elected, be appointed to any civil Office under the Authority of the United States, which shall have been created, or the Emoluments whereof shall have been encreased during such time; and no Person holding any Office under the United States, shall be a Member of either House during his Continuance in Office.

Section 7

All Bills for raising Revenue shall originate in the House of Representatives; but the Senate may propose or concur with Amendments as on other Bills.

Every Bill which shall have passed the House of Representatives and the Senate, shall, before it become a Law, be presented to the

President of the United States; If he approve he shall sign it, but if not he shall return it, with his Objections to that House in which it shall have originated, who shall enter the Objections at large on their Journal, and proceed to reconsider it. If after such Reconsideration two thirds of that House shall agree to pass the Bill, it shall be sent, together with the Objections, to the other House, by which it shall likewise be reconsidered, and if approved by two thirds of that House, it shall become a Law.

But in all such Cases the Votes of both Houses shall be determined by yeas and Nays, and the Names of the Persons voting for and against the Bill shall be entered on the Journal of each House respectively. If any Bill shall not be returned by the President within ten Days (Sundays excepted) after it shall have been presented to him, the Same shall be a Law, in like Manner as if he had signed it, unless the Congress by their Adjournment prevent its Return, in which Case it shall not be a Law.

Every Order, Resolution, or Vote to which the Concurrence of the Senate and House of Representatives may be necessary (except on a question of Adjournment) shall be presented to the President of the United States; and before the Same shall take Effect, shall be approved by him, or being disapproved by him, shall be repassed by two thirds of the Senate and House of Representatives, according to the Rules and Limitations prescribed in the Case of a Bill.

Section 8

The Congress shall have Power To lay and collect Taxes, Duties, Imposts and Excises, to pay the Debts and provide for the common Defence and general Welfare of the United States; but all Duties, Imposts and Excises shall be uniform throughout the United States;

To borrow Money on the credit of the United States;

To regulate Commerce with foreign Nations, and among the several States, and with the Indian Tribes;

To establish an uniform Rule of Naturalization, and uniform Laws on the subject of Bankruptcies throughout the United States;

To coin Money, regulate the Value thereof, and of foreign Coin, and fix the Standard of Weights and Measures;

To provide for the Punishment of counterfeiting the Securities and current Coin of the United States;

To establish Post Offices and post Roads;

To promote the Progress of Science and useful Arts, by securing for limited Times to Authors and Inventors the exclusive Right to their respective Writings and Discoveries;

To constitute Tribunals inferior to the supreme Court;

To define and punish Piracies and Felonies committed on the high Seas, and Offences against the Law of Nations;

To declare War, grant Letters of Marque and Reprisal, and make Rules concerning Captures on Land and Water;

To raise and support Armies, but no Appropriation of Money to that Use shall be for a longer Term than two Years;

To provide and maintain a Navy;

To make Rules for the Government and Regulation of the land and naval Forces;

To provide for calling forth the Militia to execute the Laws of the Union, suppress Insurrections and repel Invasions;

To provide for organizing, arming, and disciplining, the Militia, and for governing such Part of them as may be employed in the Service of the United States, reserving to the States respectively, the Appointment of the Officers, and the Authority of training the Militia according to the discipline prescribed by Congress;

To exercise exclusive Legislation in all Cases whatsoever, over such District (not exceeding ten Miles square) as may, by Cession of particular States, and the Acceptance of Congress, become the Seat of the Government of the United States, and to exercise like Authority over all Places purchased by the Consent of the Legislature of the State in which the Same shall be, for the Erection of Forts, Magazines, Arsenals, dock-Yards, and other needful Buildings;--And

To make all Laws which shall be necessary and proper for carrying into Execution the foregoing Powers, and all other Powers vested by this Constitution in the Government of the United States, or in any Department or Officer thereof.

Section 9

The Migration or Importation of such Persons as any of the States now existing shall think proper to admit, shall not be prohibited by the Congress prior to the Year one thousand eight hundred and eight, but a Tax or duty may be imposed on such Importation, not exceeding ten dollars for each Person.

The Privilege of the Writ of Habeas Corpus shall not be suspended, unless when in Cases of Rebellion or Invasion the public Safety may require it.

No Bill of Attainder or ex post facto Law shall be passed.

No Capitation, or other direct, Tax shall be laid, unless in Proportion to the Census or Enumeration herein before directed to be taken.

No Tax or Duty shall be laid on Articles exported from any State.

No Preference shall be given by any Regulation of Commerce or Revenue to the Ports of one State over those of another: nor shall Vessels bound to, or from, one State, be obliged to enter, clear, or pay Duties in another.

No Money shall be drawn from the Treasury, but in Consequence of Appropriations made by Law; and a regular Statement and Account of the Receipts and Expenditures of all public Money shall be published from time to time.

No Title of Nobility shall be granted by the United States: And no Person holding any Office of Profit or Trust under them, shall, without the Consent of the Congress, accept of any present, Emolument, Office, or Title, of any kind whatever, from any King, Prince, or foreign State.

Section 10

No State shall enter into any Treaty, Alliance, or Confederation; grant Letters of Marque and Reprisal; coin Money; emit Bills of Credit; make any Thing but gold and silver Coin a Tender in Payment of Debts; pass any Bill of Attainder, ex post facto Law, or Law impairing the Obligation of Contracts, or grant any Title of Nobility.

No State shall, without the Consent of the Congress, lay any Imposts or Duties on Imports or Exports, except what may be absolutely necessary for executing it's inspection Laws: and the net Produce of all Duties and Imposts, laid by any State on Imports or Exports, shall be for the Use of the Treasury of the United States; and all such Laws shall be subject to the Revision and Controul of the Congress.

No State shall, without the Consent of Congress, lay any Duty of Tonnage, keep Troops, or Ships of War in time of Peace, enter into any Agreement or Compact with another State, or with a foreign Power, or engage in War, unless actually invaded, or in such imminent Danger as will not admit of delay.

Article II

Section 1

The executive Power shall be vested in a President of the United States of America. He shall hold his Office during the Term of four Years, and, together with the Vice President, chosen for the same Term, be elected, as follows

Each State shall appoint, in such Manner as the Legislature thereof may direct, a Number of Electors, equal to the whole Number of Senators and Representatives to which the State may be entitled in the Congress: but no Senator or Representative, or Person holding an Office of Trust or Profit under the United States, shall be appointed an Elector.

The Electors shall meet in their respective States, and vote by Ballot for two Persons, of whom one at least shall not be an Inhabitant of the same State with themselves. And they shall make a List of all the Persons voted for, and of the Number of Votes for each; which List they shall sign and certify, and transmit sealed to the Seat of the Government of the United States, directed to the President of the Senate. The President of the Senate shall, in the Presence of the Senate and House of Representatives, open all the Certificates, and the Votes shall then be counted. The Person having the greatest Number of Votes shall be the President, if such Number be a Majority of the whole Number of Electors appointed; and if there be more than one who have such Majority, and have an equal Number of Votes, then the House of Representatives shall immediately chuse by Ballot one of them for President; and if no

Person have a Majority, then from the five highest on the List the said House shall in like Manner chuse the President. But in chusing the President, the Votes shall be taken by States, the Representation from each State having one Vote; A quorum for this Purpose shall consist of a Member or Members from two thirds of the States, and a Majority of all the States shall be necessary to a Choice. In every Case, after the Choice of the President, the Person having the greatest Number of Votes of the Electors shall be the Vice President. But if there should remain two or more who have equal Votes, the Senate shall chuse from them by Ballot the Vice President.

The Congress may determine the Time of chusing the Electors, and the Day on which they shall give their Votes; which Day shall be the same throughout the United States.

No Person except a natural born Citizen, or a Citizen of the United States, at the time of the Adoption of this Constitution, shall be eligible to the Office of President; neither shall any Person be eligible to that Office who shall not have attained to the Age of thirty five Years, and been fourteen Years a Resident within the United States.

In Case of the Removal of the President from Office, or of his Death, Resignation, or Inability to discharge the Powers and Duties of the said Office, the Same shall devolve on the Vice President, and the Congress may by Law provide for the Case of Removal, Death, Resignation or Inability, both of the President and Vice President, declaring what Officer shall then act as President, and such Officer shall act accordingly, until the Disability be removed, or a President shall be elected.

The President shall, at stated Times, receive for his Services, a Compensation, which shall neither be increased nor diminished during the Period for which he shall have been elected, and he shall not receive within that Period any other Emolument from the United States, or any of them.

Before he enter on the Execution of his Office, he shall take the following Oath or Affirmation—"I do solemnly swear (or affirm) that I will faithfully execute the Office of President of the United States, and will to the best of my Ability, preserve, protect and defend the Constitution of the United States."

Section 2

The President shall be Commander in Chief of the Army and Navy of the United States, and of the Militia of the several States, when called into the actual Service of the United States; he may require the Opinion, in writing, of the principal Officer in each of the executive Departments, upon any Subject relating to the Duties of their respective Offices, and he shall have Power to grant Reprieves and Pardons for Offences against the United States, except in Cases of Impeachment.

He shall have Power, by and with the Advice and Consent of the Senate, to make Treaties, provided two thirds of the Senators present concur; and he shall nominate, and by and with the Advice and Consent of the Senate, shall appoint Ambassadors, other public Ministers and Consuls, Judges of the supreme Court, and all other Officers of the United States, whose Appointments are not herein otherwise provided for, and which shall be established by Law: but the Congress may by Law vest the Appointment of such inferior Officers, as they think proper, in the President alone, in the Courts of Law, or in the Heads of Departments.

The President shall have Power to fill up all Vacancies that may happen during the Recess of the Senate, by granting Commissions which shall expire at the End of their next Session.

Section 3

He shall from time to time give to the Congress Information of the State of the Union, and recommend to their Consideration such Measures as he shall judge necessary and expedient; he may, on extraordinary Occasions, convene both Houses, or either of them, and in Case of Disagreement between them, with Respect to the Time of Adjournment, he may adjourn them to such Time as he shall think proper; he shall receive Ambassadors and other public Ministers; he shall take Care that the Laws be faithfully executed, and shall Commission all the Officers of the United States.

Section 4

The President, Vice President and all civil Officers of the United States, shall be removed from Office on Impeachment for, and Conviction of, Treason, Bribery, or other high Crimes and Misdemeanors.

Article III

Section 1

The judicial Power of the United States, shall be vested in one supreme Court, and in such inferior Courts as the Congress may from time to time ordain and establish. The Judges, both of the supreme and inferior Courts, shall hold their Offices during good Behaviour, and shall, at stated Times, receive for their Services, a Compensation, which shall not be diminished during their Continuance in Office.

Section 2

The judicial Power shall extend to all Cases, in Law and Equity, arising under this Constitution, the Laws of the United States, and Treaties made, or which shall be made, under their Authority;–to all Cases affecting Ambassadors, other public Ministers and Consuls;–to all Cases of admiralty and maritime Jurisdiction;–to Controversies to which the United States shall be a Party;–to Controversies between two or more States;–between a State and Citizens of another State; –between Citizens of different States, –between Citizens of the same State claiming Lands under Grants of different States, and between a State, or the Citizens thereof, and foreign States, Citizens or Subjects.

In all Cases affecting Ambassadors, other public Ministers and Consuls, and those in which a State shall be Party, the supreme Court shall have original Jurisdiction. In all the other Cases before mentioned, the supreme Court shall have appellate Jurisdiction, both as to Law and Fact, with such Exceptions, and under such Regulations as the Congress shall make.

The Trial of all Crimes, except in Cases of Impeachment, shall be by Jury; and such Trial shall be held in the State where the said

Crimes shall have been committed; but when not committed within any State, the Trial shall be at such Place or Places as the Congress may by Law have directed.

Section 3

Treason against the United States, shall consist only in levying War against them, or in adhering to their Enemies, giving them Aid and Comfort. No Person shall be convicted of Treason unless on the Testimony of two Witnesses to the same overt Act, or on Confession in open Court.

The Congress shall have Power to declare the Punishment of Treason, but no Attainder of Treason shall work Corruption of Blood, or Forfeiture except during the Life of the Person attainted.

Article IV

Section 1

Full Faith and Credit shall be given in each State to the public Acts, Records, and judicial Proceedings of every other State. And the Congress may by general Laws prescribe the Manner in which such Acts, Records and Proceedings shall be proved, and the Effect thereof.

Section 2

The Citizens of each State shall be entitled to all Privileges and Immunities of Citizens in the several States.

A Person charged in any State with Treason, Felony, or other Crime, who shall flee from Justice, and be found in another State, shall on Demand of the executive Authority of the State from which he fled, be delivered up, to be removed to the State having Jurisdiction of the Crime.

No Person held to Service or Labour in one State, under the Laws thereof, escaping into another, shall, in Consequence of any Law or Regulation therein, be discharged from such Service or Labour, but shall be delivered up on Claim of the Party to whom such Service or Labour may be due.

Section 3

New States may be admitted by the Congress into this Union; but no new State shall be formed or erected within the Jurisdiction of any other State; nor any State be formed by the Junction of two or more States, or Parts of States, without the Consent of the Legislatures of the States concerned as well as of the Congress.

The Congress shall have Power to dispose of and make all needful Rules and Regulations respecting the Territory or other Property belonging to the United States; and nothing in this Constitution shall be so construed as to Prejudice any Claims of the United States, or of any particular State.

Section 4

The United States shall guarantee to every State in this Union a Republican Form of Government, and shall protect each of them against Invasion; and on Application of the Legislature, or of the Executive (when the Legislature cannot be convened) against domestic Violence.

Article V

The Congress, whenever two thirds of both Houses shall deem it necessary, shall propose Amendments to this Constitution, or, on the Application of the Legislatures of two thirds of the several States, shall call a Convention for proposing Amendments, which, in either Case, shall be valid to all Intents and Purposes, as Part of this Constitution, when ratified by the Legislatures of three fourths of the several States, or by Conventions in three fourths thereof, as the one or the other Mode of Ratification may be proposed by the Congress; Provided that no Amendment which may be made prior to the Year One thousand eight hundred and eight shall in any Manner affect the first and fourth Clauses in the

Ninth Section of the first Article; and that no State, without its Consent, shall be deprived of its equal Suffrage in the Senate.

Article VI

All Debts contracted and Engagements entered into, before the Adoption of this Constitution, shall be as valid against the United States under this Constitution, as under the Confederation.

This Constitution, and the Laws of the United States which shall be made in Pursuance thereof; and all Treaties made, or which shall be made, under the Authority of the United States, shall be the supreme Law of the Land; and the Judges in every State shall be bound thereby, any Thing in the Constitution or Laws of any State to the Contrary notwithstanding.

The Senators and Representatives before mentioned, and the Members of the several State Legislatures, and all executive and judicial Officers, both of the United States and of the several States, shall be bound by Oath or Affirmation, to support this Constitution; but no religious Test shall ever be required as a Qualification to any Office or public Trust under the United States.

Article VII

The Ratification of the Conventions of nine States, shall be sufficient for the Establishment of this Constitution between the States so ratifying the Same.

The Word "the," being interlined between the seventh and eight Lines of the first Page, The Word "Thirty" being partly written on an Erazure in the fifteenth Line of the first Page. The Words "is tried" being interlined between the thirty second and thirty third Lines of the first Page and the Word "the" being interlined between the forty third and forty fourth Lines of the second Page.

done in Convention by the Unanimous Consent of the States present the Seventeenth Day of September in the Year of our Lord one thousand seven hundred and Eighty seven and of the Independence of the United States of America the Twelfth In witness whereof We have hereunto subscribed our Names,

Attest William Jackson Secretary

Go: Washington -Presidt. and deputy from Virginia

Delaware:
    Geo: Read, Gunning Bedford jun, John Dickinson
    Richard Bassett, Jaco: Broom
Maryland:
    James McHenry, Dan of St, Thos. Jenifer, Danl Carroll.
Virginia:
    John Blair, James Madison Jr.
North Carolina:
    Wm Blount, Richd. Dobbs Spaight, Hu Williamson
South Carolina:
    J. Rutledge, Charles Cotesworth Pinckney, Charles Pinckney
    Pierce Butler.
Georgia:
    William Few, Abr Baldwin
New Hampshire:
    John Langdon, Nicholas Gilman
Massachusetts:
    Nathaniel Gorham, Rufus King
Connecticut:
    Wm. Saml. Johnson, Roger Sherman
New York:
    Alexander Hamilton
New Jersey:
    Wil. Livingston, David Brearley, Wm. Paterson, Jona: Dayton
Pennsylvania
    B Franklin, Thomas Mifflin, Robt Morris, Geo. Clymer
    Thos. FitzSimons, Jared Ingersoll, James Wilson.
    Gouv Morris

Preamble

Congress of the United States begun and held at the City of New-York, on Wednesday the fourth of March, one thousand seven hundred and eighty nine.

THE Conventions of a number of the States, having at the time of their adopting the Constitution, expressed a desire, in order to prevent misconstruction or abuse of its powers, that further declaratory and restrictive clauses should be added: And as extending the ground of public confidence in the Government, will best ensure the beneficent ends of its institution.

RESOLVED by the Senate and House of Representatives of the United States of America, in Congress assembled, two thirds of both Houses concurring, that the following Articles be proposed to the Legislatures of the several States, as amendments to the Constitution of the United States, all, or any of which Articles, when ratified by three fourths of the said Legislatures, to be valid to all intents and purposes, as part of the said Constitution; viz.

ARTICLES in addition to, and Amendment of the Constitution of the United States of America, proposed by Congress, and ratified by the Legislatures of the several States, pursuant to the fifth Article of the original Constitution.

(Articles I through X are known as the Bill of Rights)

AMENDMENT I

Congress shall make no law respecting an establishment of religion, or prohibiting the free exercise thereof; or abridging the freedom of speech, or of the press, or the right of the people peaceably to assemble, and to petition the Government for a redress of grievances.

AMENDMENT II

A well regulated Militia, being necessary to the security of a free State, the right of the people to keep and bear Arms, shall not be infringed.

AMENDMENT III

No Soldier shall, in time of peace be quartered in any house, without the consent of the Owner; nor in time of war, but in a manner to be prescribed by law.

AMENDMENT IV

The right of the people to be secure in their persons, houses, papers, and effects, against unreasonable searches and seizures, shall not be violated, and no Warrants shall issue, but upon probable cause, supported by Oath or affirmation, and particularly describing the place to be searched, and the persons or things to be seized.

AMENDMENT V

No person shall be held to answer for a capital, or otherwise infamous crime, unless on a presentment or indictment of a Grand Jury, except in cases arising in the land or naval forces, or in the Militia, when in actual service in time of War or public danger; nor shall any person be subject for the same offence to be twice put in jeopardy of life or limb; nor shall be compelled in any criminal case to be a witness against himself; nor be deprived of life, liberty, or property, without due process of law; nor shall private property be taken for public use without just compensation.

AMENDMENT VI

In all criminal prosecutions, the accused shall enjoy the right to a speedy and public trial, by an impartial jury of the State and district wherein the crime shall have been committed; which district shall have been previously ascertained by law, and to be informed of the nature and cause of the accusation; to be confronted with the witnesses against him; to have compulsory process for obtaining witnesses in his favor; and to have the assistance of counsel for his defence.

AMENDMENT VII

In Suits at common law, where the value in controversy shall exceed twenty dollars, the right of trial by jury shall be preserved, and no fact tried by a jury shall be otherwise reexamined in any Court of the United States, than according to the rules of common law.

AMENDMENT VIII

Excessive bail shall not be required, nor excessive fines imposed, nor cruel and unusual punishments inflicted.

AMENDMENT IX

The enumeration in the Constitution of certain rights shall not be construed to deny or disparage others retained by the people.

AMENDMENT X

The powers not delegated to the United States by the Constitution, nor prohibited by it to the States, are reserved to the States respectively, or to the people.

AMENDMENT XI
Passed by Congress March 4, 1794. Ratified February 7, 1795.

The Judicial power of the United States shall not be construed to extend to any suit in law or equity, commenced or prosecuted against one of the United States by Citizens of another State, or by Citizens or Subjects of any Foreign State.

AMENDMENT XII
Passed by Congress December 9, 1803. Ratified June 15, 1804.

The Electors shall meet in their respective states and vote by ballot for President and Vice-President, one of whom, at least, shall not be an inhabitant of the same state with themselves; they shall name in their ballots the person voted for as President, and in distinct ballots the person voted for as Vice-President, and they shall make distinct lists of all persons voted for as President, and of all persons voted for as Vice-President, and of the number of votes for each, which lists they shall sign and certify, and transmit sealed to the seat of the government of the United States, directed to the President of the Senate; -- the President of the Senate shall, in the presence of the Senate and House of Representatives, open all the certificates and the votes shall then be counted; --

The person having the greatest number of votes for President, shall be the President, if such number be a majority of the whole number of Electors appointed; and if no person have such majority, then from the persons having the highest numbers not exceeding three on the list of those voted for as President, the House of Representatives shall choose immediately, by ballot, the President. But in choosing the President, the votes shall be taken by states, the representation from each state having one vote; a quorum for this purpose shall consist of a member or members from two-thirds of the states, and a majority of all the states shall be necessary to a choice. And if the House of Representatives shall not choose a President whenever the right of choice shall devolve upon them, before the fourth day of March next following, then the Vice-President shall act as President, as in case of the death or other constitutional disability of the President. The person having the greatest number of votes as Vice-President, shall be the Vice-President, if such number be a majority of the whole number of Electors appointed, and if no person have a majority, then from the two highest numbers on the list, the Senate shall choose the Vice-President; a quorum for the purpose shall consist of two-thirds of the whole number of Senators, and a majority of the whole number shall be necessary to a choice. But no person constitutionally ineligible to the office of President shall be eligible to that of Vice-President of the United States.

AMENDMENT XIII
Passed by Congress January 31, 1865. Ratified December 6, 1865.

Section 1. Neither slavery nor involuntary servitude, except as a punishment for crime whereof the party shall have been duly convicted, shall exist within the United States, or any place subject to their jurisdiction.

Section 2. Congress shall have power to enforce this article by appropriate legislation.

AMENDMENT XIV
Passed by Congress June 13, 1866. Ratified July 9, 1868.

Section 1. All persons born or naturalized in the United States, and subject to the jurisdiction thereof, are citizens of the United States and of the State wherein they reside. No State shall make or enforce any law which shall abridge the privileges or immunities of citizens of the United States; nor shall any State deprive any person of life, liberty, or property, without due process of law; nor deny to any person within its jurisdiction the equal protection of the laws.

Section 2. Representatives shall be apportioned among the several States according to their respective numbers, counting the whole number of persons in each State, excluding Indians not taxed. But when the right to vote at any election for the choice of electors for President and Vice-President of the United States, Representatives in Congress, the Executive and Judicial officers of a State, or the members of the Legislature thereof, is denied to any of the male inhabitants of such State, being twenty-one years of age, and citizens of the United States, or in any way abridged, except for participation in rebellion, or other crime, the basis of representation therein shall be reduced in the proportion which the number of such male citizens shall bear to the whole number of male citizens twenty-one years of age in such State.

Section 3. No person shall be a Senator or Representative in Congress, or elector of President and Vice-President, or hold any office, civil or military, under the United States, or under any State, who, having previously taken an oath, as a member of Congress, or as an officer of the United States, or as a member of any State legislature, or as an executive or judicial officer of any State, to support the Constitution of the United States, shall have engaged in insurrection or rebellion against the same, or given aid or comfort to the enemies thereof. But Congress may by a vote of two-thirds of each House, remove such disability.

Section 4. The validity of the public debt of the United States, authorized by law, including debts incurred for payment of pensions and bounties for services in suppressing insurrection or rebellion, shall not be questioned. But neither the United States nor any State shall assume or pay any debt or obligation incurred in aid of insurrection or rebellion against the United States, or any claim for the loss or emancipation of any slave; but all such debts, obligations and claims shall be held illegal and void.

Section 5. The Congress shall have the power to enforce, by appropriate legislation, the provisions of this article.

AMENDMENT XV
Passed by Congress February 26, 1869. Ratified February 3, 1870.

Section 1. The right of citizens of the United States to vote shall not be denied or abridged by the United States or by any State on account of race, color, or previous condition of servitude--

Section 2. The Congress shall have the power to enforce this article by appropriate legislation.

AMENDMENT XVI
Passed by Congress July 2, 1909. Ratified February 3, 1913.

The Congress shall have power to lay and collect taxes on incomes, from whatever source derived, without apportionment among the several States, and without regard to any census or enumeration.

AMENDMENT XVII

Passed by Congress May 13, 1912. Ratified April 8, 1913.

The Senate of the United States shall be composed of two Senators from each State, elected by the people thereof, for six years; and each Senator shall have one vote. The electors in each State shall have the qualifications requisite for electors of the most numerous branch of the State legislatures.

When vacancies happen in the representation of any State in the Senate, the executive authority of such State shall issue writs of election to fill such vacancies: Provided, That the legislature of any State may empower the executive thereof to make temporary appointments until the people fill the vacancies by election as the legislature may direct.

This amendment shall not be so construed as to affect the election or term of any Senator chosen before it becomes valid as part of the Constitution.

AMENDMENT XVIII

Passed by Congress December 18, 1917. Ratified January 16, 1919. Repealed by amendment 21.

Section 1. After one year from the ratification of this article the manufacture, sale, or transportation of intoxicating liquors within, the importation thereof into, or the exportation thereof from the United States and all territory subject to the jurisdiction thereof for beverage purposes is hereby prohibited.

Section 2. The Congress and the several States shall have concurrent power to enforce this article by appropriate legislation.

Section 3. This article shall be inoperative unless it shall have been ratified as an amendment to the Constitution by the legislatures of the several States, as provided in the Constitution, within seven years from the date of the submission hereof to the States by the Congress.

AMENDMENT XIX
Passed by Congress June 4, 1919. Ratified August 18, 1920.

The right of citizens of the United States to vote shall not be denied or abridged by the United States or by any State on account of sex.

Congress shall have power to enforce this article by appropriate legislation.

AMENDMENT XX
Passed by Congress March 2, 1932. Ratified January 23, 1933.

Section 1. The terms of the President and the Vice President shall end at noon on the 20th day of January, and the terms of Senators and Representatives at noon on the 3rd day of January, of the years in which such terms would have ended if this article had not been ratified; and the terms of their successors shall then begin.

Section 2. The Congress shall assemble at least once in every year, and such meeting shall begin at noon on the 3d day of January, unless they shall by law appoint a different day.

Section 3. If, at the time fixed for the beginning of the term of the President, the President elect shall have died, the Vice President elect shall become President. If a President shall not have been chosen before the time fixed for the beginning of his term, or if the President elect shall have failed to qualify, then the Vice President elect shall act as President until a President shall have qualified; and the Congress may by law provide for the case wherein neither a President elect nor a Vice President shall have qualified, declaring who shall then act as President, or the manner in which one who is to act shall be selected, and such person shall act accordingly until a President or Vice President shall have qualified.

Section 4. The Congress may by law provide for the case of the death of any of the persons from whom the House of Representatives may choose a President whenever the right of choice shall have devolved upon them, and for the case of the death of any of the persons from whom the Senate may choose a Vice President whenever the right of choice shall have devolved upon them.

Section 5. Sections 1 and 2 shall take effect on the 15th day of October following the ratification of this article.

Section 6. This article shall be inoperative unless it shall have been ratified as an amendment to the Constitution by the legislatures of three-fourths of the several States within seven years from the date of its submission.

AMENDMENT XXI

Passed by Congress February 20, 1933. Ratified December 5, 1933.

Section 1. The eighteenth article of amendment to the Constitution of the United States is hereby repealed.

Section 2. The transportation or importation into any State, Territory, or Possession of the United States for delivery or use therein of intoxicating liquors, in violation of the laws thereof, is hereby prohibited.

Section 3. This article shall be inoperative unless it shall have been ratified as an amendment to the Constitution by conventions in the several States, as provided in the Constitution, within seven years from the date of the submission hereof to the States by the Congress.

AMENDMENT XXII

Passed by Congress March 21, 1947. Ratified February 27, 1951.

Section 1. No person shall be elected to the office of the President more than twice, and no person who has held the office of President, or acted as President, for more than two years of a term to which some other person was elected President shall be elected to the office of President more than once. But this Article shall not apply to any person holding the office of President when this Article was proposed by Congress, and shall not prevent any person who may be holding the office of President, or acting as President, during the term within which this Article becomes operative from holding the office of President or acting as President during the remainder of such term.

Section 2. This article shall be inoperative unless it shall have been ratified as an amendment to the Constitution by the legislatures of three-fourths of the several States within seven years from the date of its submission to the States by the Congress.

AMENDMENT XXIII
Passed by Congress June 16, 1960. Ratified March 29, 1961.

Section 1. The District constituting the seat of Government of the United States shall appoint in such manner as Congress may direct:

A number of electors of President and Vice President equal to the whole number of Senators and Representatives in Congress to which the District would be entitled if it were a State, but in no event more than the least populous State; they shall be in addition to those appointed by the States, but they shall be considered, for the purposes of the election of President and Vice President, to be electors appointed by a State; and they shall meet in the District and perform such duties as provided by the twelfth article of amendment.

Section 2. The Congress shall have power to enforce this article by appropriate legislation.

AMENDMENT XXIV
Passed by Congress August 27, 1962. Ratified January 23, 1964.

Section 1. The right of citizens of the United States to vote in any primary or other election for President or Vice President, for electors for President or Vice President, or for Senator or Representative in Congress, shall not be denied or abridged by the United States or any State by reason of failure to pay any poll tax or other tax.

Section 2. The Congress shall have power to enforce this article by appropriate legislation.

AMENDMENT XXV
Passed by Congress July 6, 1965. Ratified February 10, 1967.

Section 1. In case of the removal of the President from office or of his death or resignation, the Vice President shall become President.

Section 2. Whenever there is a vacancy in the office of the Vice President, the President shall nominate a Vice President who shall take office upon confirmation by a majority vote of both Houses of Congress.

Section 3. Whenever the President transmits to the President pro tempore of the Senate and the Speaker of the House of Representatives his written declaration that he is unable to discharge the powers and duties of his office, and until he transmits to them a written declaration to the contrary, such powers and duties shall be discharged by the Vice President as Acting President.

Section 4. Whenever the Vice President and a majority of either the principal officers of the executive departments or of such other body as Congress may by law provide, transmit to the President pro tempore of the Senate and the Speaker of the House of Representatives their written declaration that the President is unable to discharge the powers and duties of his office, the Vice President shall immediately assume the powers and duties of the office as Acting President.

Thereafter, when the President transmits to the President pro tempore of the Senate and the Speaker of the House of Representatives his written declaration that no inability exists, he shall resume the powers and duties of his office unless the Vice President and a majority of either the principal officers of the executive department or of such other body as Congress may by law provide, transmit within four days to the President pro tempore of the Senate and the Speaker of the House of Representatives their written declaration that the President is unable to discharge the powers and duties of his office. Thereupon Congress shall decide the issue, assembling within forty-eight hours for that purpose if not in session. If the Congress, within twenty-one days after receipt of the latter written declaration, or, if Congress is not in session, within twenty-one days after Congress is required to assemble, determines by two-thirds vote of both Houses that the President is unable to discharge the powers and duties of his office, the Vice President shall continue to discharge the same as Acting President; otherwise, the President shall resume the powers and duties of his office.

AMENDMENT XXVI

Passed by Congress March 23, 1971. Ratified July 1, 1971.

Section 1. The right of citizens of the United States, who are eighteen years of age or older, to vote shall not be denied or abridged by the United States or by any State on account of age.

Section 2. The Congress shall have power to enforce this article by appropriate legislation.

AMENDMENT XXVII

Originally proposed Sept. 25, 1789. Ratified May 7, 1992.

No law, varying the compensation for the services of the Senators and Representatives, shall take effect, until an election of representatives shall have intervened.

APPENDIX III

WASHINGTON'S FAREWELL ADDRESS OF 1796

Friends and Citizens:

The period for a new election of a citizen to administer the executive government of the United States being not far distant, and the time actually arrived when your thoughts must be employed in designating the person who is to be clothed with that important trust, it appears to me proper, especially as it may conduce to a more distinct expression of the public voice, that I should now apprise you of the resolution I have formed, to decline being considered among the number of those out of whom a choice is to be made.

I beg you, at the same time, to do me the justice to be assured that this resolution has not been taken without a strict regard to all the considerations appertaining to the relation which binds a dutiful citizen to his country; and that in withdrawing the tender of service, which silence in my situation might imply, I am influenced by no diminution of zeal for your future interest, no deficiency of grateful respect for your past kindness, but am supported by a full conviction that the step is compatible with both.

The acceptance of, and continuance hitherto in, the office to which your suffrages have twice called me have been a uniform sacrifice of inclination to the opinion of duty and to a deference for what appeared to be your desire. I constantly hoped that it would have been much earlier in my power, consistently with motives which I was not at liberty to disregard, to return to that retirement from which I had been reluctantly drawn. The strength of my inclination to do this, previous to the last election, had even led to the preparation of an address to declare it to you; but mature reflection on the then perplexed and critical posture of our affairs with foreign nations, and the unanimous advice of persons entitled to my confidence, impelled me to abandon the idea.

I rejoice that the state of your concerns, external as well as internal, no longer renders the pursuit of inclination incompatible with the sentiment of duty or propriety, and am persuaded, whatever partiality may be retained for my services, that, in the present circumstances of our country, you will not disapprove my determination to retire.

The impressions with which I first undertook the arduous trust were explained on the proper occasion. In the discharge of this trust, I will only say that I have, with good intentions, contributed towards the organization and administration of the government the best exertions of which a very fallible judgment was capable. Not unconscious in the outset of the inferiority of my qualifications, experience in my own eyes, perhaps still more in the eyes of others, has strengthened the motives to diffidence of myself; and every day the increasing weight of years admonishes me more and more that the shade of retirement is as necessary to me as it will be welcome. Satisfied that if any circumstances have given peculiar value to my services, they were temporary, I have the consolation to believe that, while choice and prudence invite me to quit the political scene, patriotism does not forbid it.

In looking forward to the moment which is intended to terminate the career of my public life, my feelings do not permit me to suspend the deep acknowledgment of that debt of gratitude which I owe to my beloved country for the many honors it has conferred upon me; still more for the steadfast confidence with which it has supported me; and for the opportunities I have thence enjoyed of manifesting my inviolable attachment, by services faithful and persevering, though in usefulness unequal to my zeal. If benefits have resulted to our country from these services, let it always be remembered to your praise, and as an instructive example in our annals, that under circumstances in which the passions, agitated in every direction, were liable to mislead, amidst appearances sometimes dubious, vicissitudes of fortune often discouraging, in situations in which not unfrequently want of success has countenanced the spirit of criticism, the constancy of your support was the essential prop of the efforts, and a guarantee of the plans by which they were effected. Profoundly penetrated with this idea, I shall carry it with me to my grave, as a strong incitement to unceasing vows that heaven may continue to you the choicest tokens of its beneficence; that your union and brotherly affection may be perpetual; that the free Constitution, which is the work of your hands, may be sacredly maintained; that its administration in every department may be stamped with wisdom and virtue; that, in fine, the happiness of the people of these States, under the auspices of liberty, may be made complete by so careful a preservation and so prudent a use of this blessing as will acquire to them the glory of recommending it to the applause, the affection, and adoption of every nation which is yet a stranger to it.

Here, perhaps, I ought to stop. But a solicitude for your welfare, which cannot end but with my life, and the apprehension of danger, natural to that solicitude, urge me, on an occasion like the present, to offer to your solemn contemplation, and to recommend to your frequent review, some sentiments which are the result of much reflection, of no inconsiderable observation, and which appear to me all-important to the permanency of your felicity as a people. These will be offered to you with the more freedom, as you can only see in them the disinterested warnings of a parting friend, who can possibly have no personal motive to bias his counsel. Nor can I forget, as an encouragement to it, your indulgent reception of my sentiments on a former and not dissimilar occasion.

Interwoven as is the love of liberty with every ligament of your hearts, no recommendation of mine is necessary to fortify or confirm the attachment.

The unity of government which constitutes you one people is also now dear to you. It is justly so, for it is a main pillar in the edifice of your real independence, the support of your tranquility at home, your peace abroad; of your safety; of your prosperity; of that very liberty which you so highly prize. But as it is easy to foresee that, from different causes and from different quarters, much pains will be taken, many artifices employed to weaken in your minds the conviction of this truth; as this is the point in your political fortress against which the batteries of internal and external enemies will be most constantly and actively (though often covertly and insidiously) directed, it is of infinite moment that you should properly estimate the immense value of your national union to your collective and individual happiness; that you should cherish a cordial, habitual, and immovable attachment to it; accustoming yourselves to think and speak of it as of the palladium of your political safety and prosperity; watching for its preservation with jealous anxiety; discountenancing whatever may suggest even a suspicion that it can in any event be abandoned; and indignantly frowning upon the first dawning of every attempt to alienate any portion of our country from the rest, or to enfeeble the sacred ties which now link together the various parts.

For this you have every inducement of sympathy and interest. Citizens, by birth or choice, of a common country, that country has a right to concentrate your affections. The name of American, which belongs to you in your national capacity, must always exalt the just pride of patriotism more than any appellation derived from local discriminations. With slight shades of difference, you have the same religion, manners, habits, and political principles. You have in a common cause fought and triumphed together; the independence and liberty you possess are the work of joint counsels, and joint efforts of common dangers, sufferings, and successes.

But these considerations, however powerfully they address themselves to your sensibility, are greatly outweighed by those which apply more immediately to your interest. Here every portion of our country finds the most commanding motives for carefully guarding and preserving the union of the whole.

The North, in an unrestrained intercourse with the South, protected by the equal laws of a common government, finds in the productions of the latter great additional resources of maritime and commercial enterprise and precious materials of manufacturing industry. The South, in the same intercourse, benefiting by the agency of the North, sees its agriculture grow and its commerce expand. Turning partly into its own channels the seamen of the North, it finds its particular navigation invigorated; and, while it contributes, in different ways, to nourish and increase the general mass of the national navigation, it looks forward to the protection of a maritime strength, to which itself is unequally adapted. The East, in a like intercourse with the West, already finds, and in the progressive improvement of interior communications by land and water, will more and more find a valuable vent for the commodities which it brings from abroad, or manufactures at home. The West derives from the East supplies requisite to its growth and comfort, and, what is perhaps of still greater consequence, it must of necessity owe the secure enjoyment of indispensable outlets for its own productions to the weight, influence, and the future maritime strength of the Atlantic side of the Union, directed by an indissoluble community of interest as one nation. Any other tenure by which the West can hold this essential advantage, whether derived from its own separate strength, or from an apostate and unnatural connection with any foreign power, must be intrinsically precarious.

While, then, every part of our country thus feels an immediate and particular interest in union, all the parts combined cannot fail to find in the united mass of means and efforts greater strength, greater resource, proportionably greater security from external danger, a less frequent interruption of their peace by foreign nations; and, what is of inestimable value, they must derive from union an exemption from those broils and wars between themselves, which so frequently afflict neighboring countries not tied together by the same governments, which their own rival ships alone would be sufficient to produce, but which opposite foreign alliances, attachments, and intrigues would stimulate and embitter. Hence, likewise, they will avoid the necessity of those overgrown military establishments which, under any form of government, are inauspicious to liberty, and which are to be regarded as particularly hostile to republican liberty. In this sense it is that your union ought to be considered as a main prop of your liberty, and that the love of the one ought to endear to you the preservation of the other.

These considerations speak a persuasive language to every reflecting and virtuous mind, and exhibit the continuance of the Union as a primary object of patriotic desire. Is there a doubt whether a common government can embrace so large a sphere? Let experience solve it. To listen to mere speculation in such a case were criminal. We are authorized to hope that a proper organization of the whole with the auxiliary agency of governments for the respective subdivisions, will afford a happy issue to the experiment. It is well worth a fair and full experiment. With such powerful and obvious motives to union, affecting all parts of our country, while experience shall not have demonstrated its impracticability, there will always be reason to distrust the patriotism of those who in any quarter may endeavor to weaken its bands.

In contemplating the causes which may disturb our Union, it occurs as matter of serious concern that any ground should have been furnished for characterizing parties by geographical discriminations, Northern and Southern, Atlantic and Western; whence designing men may endeavor to excite a belief that there is a real difference of local interests and views. One of the expedients of party to acquire influence within particular districts is to misrepresent the opinions and aims of other districts. You cannot shield yourselves too much against the jealousies and heartburnings which spring from these misrepresentations; they tend to render alien to each other those who ought to be bound together by fraternal affection. The inhabitants of our Western country have lately had a useful lesson on this head; they have seen, in the negotiation by the Executive, and in the unanimous ratification by the Senate, of the treaty with Spain, and in the universal satisfaction at that event, throughout the United States, a decisive proof how unfounded were the suspicions propagated among them of a policy in the General Government and in the Atlantic States unfriendly to their interests in regard to the Mississippi; they have been witnesses to the formation of two treaties, that with Great Britain, and that with Spain, which secure to them everything they could desire, in respect to our foreign relations, towards confirming their prosperity. Will it not be their wisdom to rely for the preservation of these advantages on the Union by which they were procured ? Will they not henceforth be deaf to those advisers, if such there are, who would sever them from their brethren and connect them with aliens?

To the efficacy and permanency of your Union, a government for the whole is indispensable. No alliance, however strict, between the parts can be an adequate substitute; they must inevitably experience the infractions and interruptions which all alliances in all times have experienced. Sensible of this momentous truth, you have improved upon your first essay, by the adoption of a constitution of government better calculated than your former for an intimate union, and for the efficacious management of your common concerns. This government, the offspring of our own choice, uninfluenced and unawed, adopted upon full investigation and mature deliberation, completely free in its principles, in the distribution of its powers, uniting security with energy, and containing within itself a provision for its own amendment, has a just claim to your confidence and your support. Respect for its authority, compliance with its laws, acquiescence in its measures, are duties enjoined by the fundamental maxims of true liberty. The basis of our political systems is the right of the people to make and to alter their constitutions of government. But the Constitution which at any time exists, till changed by an explicit and authentic act of the whole people, is sacredly obligatory upon all. The very idea of the power and the right of the people to establish government presupposes the duty of every individual to obey the established government.

All obstructions to the execution of the laws, all combinations and associations, under whatever plausible character, with the real design to direct, control, counteract, or awe the regular deliberation and action of the constituted authorities, are destructive of this fundamental principle, and of fatal tendency. They serve to organize faction, to give it an artificial and extraordinary force; to put, in the place of the delegated will of the nation the will of a party, often a small but artful and enterprising minority of the community; and, according to the alternate triumphs of different parties, to make the public administration the mirror of the ill-concerted and incongruous projects of faction, rather than the organ of consistent and wholesome plans digested by common counsels and modified by mutual interests.

However combinations or associations of the above description may now and then answer popular ends, they are likely, in the course of time and things, to become potent engines, by which cunning, ambitious, and unprincipled men will be enabled to subvert the power of the people and to usurp for themselves the reins of government, destroying afterwards the very engines which have lifted them to unjust dominion.

Towards the preservation of your government, and the permanency of your present happy state, it is requisite, not only that you steadily discountenance irregular oppositions to its acknowledged authority, but also that you resist with care the spirit of innovation upon its principles, however specious the pretexts. One method of assault may be to effect, in the forms of the Constitution, alterations which will impair the energy of the system, and thus to undermine what cannot be directly overthrown. In all the changes to which you may be invited, remember that time and habit are at least as necessary to fix the true character of governments as of other human institutions; that experience is the surest standard by which to test the real tendency of the existing constitution of a country; that facility in changes, upon the credit of mere hypothesis and opinion, exposes to perpetual change, from the endless variety of hypothesis and opinion; and remember, especially, that for the efficient management of your common interests, in a country so extensive as ours, a government of as much vigor as is consistent with the perfect security of liberty is indispensable. Liberty itself will find in such a government, with powers properly distributed and adjusted, its surest guardian. It is, indeed, little else than a name, where the government is too feeble to withstand the enterprises of faction, to confine each member of the society within the limits prescribed by the laws, and to maintain all in the secure and tranquil enjoyment of the rights of person and property.

I have already intimated to you the danger of parties in the State, with particular reference to the founding of them on geographical discriminations. Let me now take a more comprehensive view, and warn you in the most solemn manner against the baneful effects of the spirit of party generally.

This spirit, unfortunately, is inseparable from our nature, having its root in the strongest passions of the human mind. It exists under different shapes in all governments, more or less stifled, controlled, or repressed; but, in those of the popular form, it is seen in its greatest rankness, and is truly their worst enemy.

The alternate domination of one faction over another, sharpened by the spirit of revenge, natural to party dissension, which in different ages and countries has perpetrated the most horrid enormities, is itself a frightful despotism. But this leads at length to a more formal and permanent despotism. The disorders and miseries which result gradually incline the minds of men to seek security and repose in the absolute power of an individual; and sooner or later the chief of some prevailing faction, more able or more fortunate than his competitors, turns this disposition to the purposes of his own elevation, on the ruins of public liberty.

Without looking forward to an extremity of this kind (which nevertheless ought not to be entirely out of sight), the common and continual mischiefs of the spirit of party are sufficient to make it the interest and duty of a wise people to discourage and restrain it.

It serves always to distract the public councils and enfeeble the public administration. It agitates the community with ill-founded jealousies and false alarms, kindles the animosity of one part against another, foments occasionally riot and insurrection. It opens the door to foreign influence and corruption, which finds a facilitated access to the government itself through the channels of party passions. Thus the policy and the will of one country are subjected to the policy and will of another.

There is an opinion that parties in free countries are useful checks upon the administration of the government and serve to keep alive the spirit of liberty. This within certain limits is probably true; and in governments of a monarchical cast, patriotism may look with indulgence, if not with favor, upon the spirit of party. But in those of the popular character, in governments purely elective, it is a spirit not to be encouraged. From their natural tendency, it is certain there will always be enough of that spirit for every salutary purpose. And there being constant danger of excess, the effort ought to be by force of public opinion, to mitigate and assuage it. A fire not to be quenched, it demands a uniform vigilance to prevent its bursting into a flame, lest, instead of warming, it should consume.

It is important, likewise, that the habits of thinking in a free country should inspire caution in those entrusted with its administration, to confine themselves within their respective constitutional spheres, avoiding in the exercise of the powers of one department to encroach upon another. The spirit of encroachment tends to consolidate the powers of all the departments in one, and thus to create, whatever the form of government, a real despotism. A just estimate of that love of power, and proneness to abuse it, which predominates in the human heart, is sufficient to satisfy us of the truth of this position. The necessity of reciprocal checks in the exercise of political power, by dividing and distributing it into different depositaries, and constituting each the guardian of the public weal against invasions by the others, has been evinced by experiments ancient and modern; some of them in our country and under our own eyes. To preserve them must be as necessary as to institute them. If, in the opinion of the people, the distribution or modification of the constitutional powers be in any particular wrong, let it be corrected by an amendment in the way which the Constitution designates. But let there be no change by usurpation; for though this, in one instance, may be the instrument of good, it is the customary weapon by which free governments are destroyed. The precedent must always greatly overbalance in permanent evil any partial or transient benefit, which the use can at any time yield.

Of all the dispositions and habits which lead to political prosperity, religion and morality are indispensable supports. In vain would that man claim the tribute of patriotism, who should labor to subvert these great pillars of human happiness, these firmest props of the duties of men and citizens. The mere politician, equally with the pious man, ought to respect and to cherish them. A volume could not trace all their connections with private and public felicity. Let it simply be asked: Where is the security for property, for reputation, for life, if the sense of religious obligation desert the oaths which are the instruments of investigation in courts of justice ? And let us with caution indulge the supposition that morality can be maintained without religion. Whatever may be conceded to the influence of refined education on minds of peculiar structure, reason and experience both forbid us to expect that national morality can prevail in exclusion of religious principle.

It is substantially true that virtue or morality is a necessary spring of popular government. The rule, indeed, extends with more or less force to every species of free government. Who that is a sincere friend to it can look with indifference upon attempts to shake the foundation of the fabric?

Promote then, as an object of primary importance, institutions for the general diffusion of knowledge. In proportion as the structure of a government gives force to public opinion, it is essential that public opinion should be enlightened.

As a very important source of strength and security, cherish public credit. One method of preserving it is to use it as sparingly as possible, avoiding occasions of expense by cultivating peace, but remembering also that timely disbursements to prepare for danger frequently prevent much greater disbursements to repel it, avoiding likewise the accumulation of debt, not only by shunning occasions of expense, but by vigorous exertion in time of peace to discharge the debts which unavoidable wars may have occasioned, not ungenerously throwing upon posterity the burden which we ourselves ought to bear. The execution of these maxims belongs to your representatives, but it is necessary that public opinion should co-operate. To facilitate to them the performance of their duty, it is essential that you should practically bear in mind that towards the payment of debts there must be revenue; that to have revenue there must be taxes; that no taxes can be devised which are not more or less inconvenient and unpleasant; that the intrinsic embarrassment, inseparable from the selection of the proper objects (which is always a choice of difficulties), ought to be a decisive motive for a candid construction of the conduct of the government in making it, and for a spirit of acquiescence in the measures for obtaining revenue, which the public exigencies may at any time dictate.

Observe good faith and justice towards all nations; cultivate peace and harmony with all. Religion and morality enjoin this conduct; and can it be, that good policy does not equally enjoin it - It will be worthy of a free, enlightened, and at no distant period, a great nation, to give to mankind the magnanimous and too novel example of a people always guided by an exalted justice and benevolence. Who can doubt that, in the course of time and things, the fruits of such a plan would richly repay any temporary advantages which might be lost by a steady adherence to it ? Can it be that Providence has not connected the permanent felicity of a nation with its virtue ? The experiment, at least, is recommended by every sentiment which ennobles human nature. Alas! is it rendered impossible by its vices?

In the execution of such a plan, nothing is more essential than that permanent, inveterate antipathies against particular nations, and passionate attachments for others, should be excluded; and that, in place of them, just and amicable feelings towards all should be cultivated. The nation which indulges towards another a habitual hatred or a habitual fondness is in some degree a slave. It is a slave to its animosity or to its affection, either of which is sufficient to lead it astray from its duty and its interest. Antipathy in one nation against another disposes each more readily to offer insult and injury, to lay hold of slight causes of umbrage, and to be haughty and intractable, when accidental or trifling occasions of dispute occur. Hence, frequent collisions, obstinate, envenomed, and bloody contests. The nation, prompted by ill-will and resentment, sometimes impels to war the government, contrary to the best calculations of policy. The government sometimes participates in the national propensity, and adopts through passion what reason would reject; at other times it makes the animosity of the nation subservient to projects of hostility instigated by pride, ambition, and other sinister and pernicious motives. The peace often, sometimes perhaps the liberty, of nations, has been the victim.

So likewise, a passionate attachment of one nation for another produces a variety of evils. Sympathy for the favorite nation, facilitating the illusion of an imaginary common interest in cases where no real common interest exists, and infusing into one the enmities of the other, betrays the former into a participation in the quarrels and wars of the latter without adequate inducement or justification. It leads also to concessions to the favorite nation of privileges denied to others which is apt doubly to injure the nation making the concessions; by unnecessarily parting with what ought to have been retained, and by exciting jealousy, ill-will, and a disposition to retaliate, in the parties from whom equal privileges are withheld. And it gives to ambitious, corrupted, or deluded citizens (who devote themselves to the favorite nation), facility to betray or sacrifice the interests of their own country, without odium, sometimes even with popularity; gilding, with the appearances of a virtuous sense of obligation, a commendable deference for public opinion, or a laudable zeal for public good, the base or foolish compliances of ambition, corruption, or infatuation.

As avenues to foreign influence in innumerable ways, such attachments are particularly alarming to the truly enlightened and independent patriot. How many opportunities do they afford to tamper with domestic factions, to practice the arts of seduction, to mislead public opinion, to influence or awe the public councils. Such an attachment of a small or weak towards a great and powerful nation dooms the former to be the satellite of the latter.

Against the insidious wiles of foreign influence (I conjure you to believe me, fellow-citizens) the jealousy of a free people ought to be constantly awake, since history and experience prove that foreign influence is one of the most baneful foes of republican government. But that jealousy to be useful must be impartial; else it becomes the instrument of the very influence to be avoided, instead of a defense against it. Excessive partiality for one foreign nation and excessive dislike of another cause those whom they actuate to see danger only on one side, and serve to veil and even second the arts of influence on the other. Real patriots who may resist the intrigues of the favorite are liable to become suspected and odious, while its tools and dupes usurp the applause and confidence of the people, to surrender their interests.

The great rule of conduct for us in regard to foreign nations is in extending our commercial relations, to have with them as little political connection as possible. So far as we have already formed engagements, let them be fulfilled with perfect good faith. Here let us stop. Europe has a set of primary interests which to us have none; or a very remote relation. Hence she must be engaged in frequent controversies, the causes of which are essentially foreign to our concerns. Hence, therefore, it must be unwise in us to implicate ourselves by artificial ties in the ordinary vicissitudes of her politics, or the ordinary combinations and collisions of her friendships or enmities.

Our detached and distant situation invites and enables us to pursue a different course. If we remain one people under an efficient government. the period is not far off when we may defy material injury from external annoyance; when we may take such an attitude as will cause the neutrality we may at any time resolve upon to be scrupulously respected; when belligerent nations, under the impossibility of making acquisitions upon us, will not lightly hazard the giving us provocation; when we may choose peace or war, as our interest, guided by justice, shall counsel.

Why forego the advantages of so peculiar a situation? Why quit our own to stand upon foreign ground? Why, by interweaving our destiny with that of any part of Europe, entangle our peace and prosperity in the toils of European ambition, rivalship, interest, humor or caprice?

It is our true policy to steer clear of permanent alliances with any portion of the foreign world; so far, I mean, as we are now at liberty to do it; for let me not be understood as capable of patronizing infidelity to existing engagements. I hold the maxim no less applicable to public than to private affairs, that honesty is always the best policy. I repeat it, therefore, let those engagements be observed in their genuine sense. But, in my opinion, it is unnecessary and would be unwise to extend them.

Taking care always to keep ourselves by suitable establishments on a respectable defensive posture, we may safely trust to temporary alliances for extraordinary emergencies.

Harmony, liberal intercourse with all nations, are recommended by policy, humanity, and interest. But even our commercial policy should hold an equal and impartial hand; neither seeking nor granting exclusive favors or preferences; consulting the natural course of things; diffusing and diversifying by gentle means the streams of commerce, but forcing nothing; establishing (with powers so disposed, in order to give trade a stable course, to define the rights of our merchants, and to enable the government to support them) conventional rules of intercourse, the best that present circumstances and mutual opinion will permit, but temporary, and liable to be from time to time abandoned or varied, as experience and circumstances shall dictate; constantly keeping in view that it is folly in one nation to look for disinterested favors from another; that it must pay with a portion of its independence for whatever it may accept under that character; that, by such acceptance, it may place itself in the condition of having given equivalents for nominal favors, and yet of being reproached with ingratitude for not giving more. There can be no greater error than to expect or calculate upon real favors from nation to nation. It is an illusion, which experience must cure, which a just pride ought to discard.

In offering to you, my countrymen, these counsels of an old and affectionate friend, I dare not hope they will make the strong and lasting impression I could wish; that they will control the usual current of the passions, or prevent our nation from running the course which has hitherto marked the destiny of nations. But, if I may even flatter myself that they may be productive of some partial benefit, some occasional good; that they may now and then recur to moderate the fury of party spirit, to warn against the mischiefs of foreign intrigue, to guard against the impostures of pretended patriotism; this hope will be a full recompense for the solicitude for your welfare, by which they have been dictated.

How far in the discharge of my official duties I have been guided by the principles which have been delineated, the public records and other evidences of my conduct must witness to you and to the world. To myself, the assurance of my own conscience is, that I have at least believed myself to be guided by them.

In relation to the still subsisting war in Europe, my proclamation of the twenty-second of April, 1793, is the index of my plan. Sanctioned by your approving voice, and by that of your representatives in both houses of Congress, the spirit of that measure has continually governed me, uninfluenced by any attempts to deter or divert me from it.

After deliberate examination, with the aid of the best lights I could obtain, I was well satisfied that our country, under all the circumstances of the case, had a right to take, and was bound in duty and interest to take, a neutral position. Having taken it, I determined, as far as should depend upon me, to maintain it, with moderation, perseverance, and firmness.

The considerations which respect the right to hold this conduct, it is not necessary on this occasion to detail. I will only observe that, according to my understanding of the matter, that right, so far from being denied by any of the belligerent powers, has been virtually admitted by all.

The duty of holding a neutral conduct may be inferred, without anything more, from the obligation which justice and humanity impose on every nation, in cases in which it is free to act, to maintain inviolate the relations of peace and amity towards other nations.

The inducements of interest for observing that conduct will best be referred to your own reflections and experience. With me a predominant motive has been to endeavor to gain time to our country to settle and mature its yet recent institutions, and to progress without interruption to that degree of strength and consistency which is necessary to give it, humanly speaking, the command of its own fortunes.

Though, in reviewing the incidents of my administration, I am unconscious of intentional error, I am nevertheless too sensible of my defects not to think it probable that I may have committed many errors. Whatever they may be, I fervently beseech the Almighty to avert or mitigate the evils to which they may tend. I shall also carry with me the hope that my country will never cease to view them with indulgence; and that, after forty five years of my life dedicated to its service with an upright zeal, the faults of incompetent abilities will be consigned to oblivion, as myself must soon be to the mansions of rest.

Relying on its kindness in this as in other things, and actuated by that fervent love towards it, which is so natural to a man who views in it the native soil of himself and his progenitors for several generations, I anticipate with pleasing expectation that retreat in which I promise myself to realize, without alloy, the sweet enjoyment of partaking, in the midst of my fellow-citizens, the benign influence of good laws under a free government, the ever-favorite object of my heart, and the happy reward, as I trust, of our mutual cares, labors, and dangers.

INDEX

For more information
go to

www.BoomerstoMillennialstheBook.com

CPSIA information can be obtained
at www.ICGtesting.com
Printed in the USA
FFHW011727140219
50535923-55824FF